THE FRONTENAC LIBRARY
GENERAL EDITOR—GEOFFREY MILBURN
Althouse College of Education
University of Western Ontario

1. **Conscription in the Second World War, 1939-1945**
   A Study in Political Management
   J. L. Granatstein

2. **Democracy and Discontent**
   The Rise of Third Parties in the Canadian West
   Walter D. Young

3. **Guerillas and Grenadiers**
   The Struggle for Canada, 1689-1760
   I. K. Steele

   Other titles in preparation

For
J. M. S. & P. S.

Guerillas and Grenadiers
THE STRUGGLE FOR CANADA, 1689-1760

I. K. Steele

TORONTO • WINNIPEG • VANCOUVER
THE RYERSON PRESS

© THE RYERSON PRESS, 1969

All rights reserved.
No part of this book may be reproduced in any form (except by reviewers for the public press) without permission in writing from the publisher.

SBN 7700 0272 2

Acknowledgments

The Publisher wishes to acknowledge with gratitude those who have given their permission to use copyrighted material in this book.

Where necessary, permission to quote copyrighted material has been sought through the publishers noted in the relevant places.

The illustrations in this book have been obtained from the following sources:

Château de Ramezay, Montreal, p. 98.
Cumberland Map Collection, Royal Library, Windsor Castle, pp. 86, 87.
John Carter Brown Library, Brown University, pp. 47, 112.
Metropolitan Museum of Art, Bequest of Charles Allen Munn, 1924, p. 48.
Metropolitan Toronto Library Board, p. 29.
Public Archives of Canada, pp. 11, 103.
Virginia Historical Society, p. 54.

Every effort has been made to credit all sources correctly. The author and publisher will welcome information that will allow them to correct any errors or omissions.

Maps by D. Hayward.

PRINTED AND BOUND IN CANADA
BY THE RYERSON PRESS, TORONTO

Foreword

The historical record is a powerful force in contemporary life. Individuals, pressure groups and political parties appeal to it and often attempt to use it to support arguments or to justify actions. Important decisions in national affairs are affected by what is thought to have happened in the past. By interpreting this past according to the evidence available and according to accepted standards of scholarly inquiry, historians claim a special relationship to the nation.

The story of the eighteenth century is not only interesting in itself but also pertinent to current issues. When we discuss the national character or debate the country's future, almost as a matter of course we refer to events of those years in which English and French Colonies existed side by side on the mainland of North America. Yet this habit should not surprise us. In that century before 1759 each colony developed lasting characteristics of its own. All of them were influenced by changing conditions in the New World and by international rivalries in the Old. The outcome of the momentous events of that period, the fall of Quebec, is well known; the reasons are much more contentious.

Dr. Steele has cast a wide net in his study of eighteenth century North America. Like other authors in the *Frontenac Library*, he has quoted from important original sources and commented upon interpretations which differ from his own. He has watched the interplay of personalities, geographic and economic forces, military and technological changes, colonial and indian relations, and imperial rivalries. Above all, he has woven all of these threads together into a compelling interpretation of the struggle for Canada.

There is a challenge to the reader both in the technique and in the thesis of *Guerillas and Grenadiers*. Dr. Steele's approach demonstrates the importance of posing new questions to a wide range of evidence. His arguments show the need for continuous reappraisal of older views. His topic is part of the origins of the nation and his findings are a contribution to on-going debates concerning Canada's identity.

G.M.

Contents

	Acknowledgments	iv
	Foreword	v
	Introduction	1
PART ONE	FRONTIERSMEN AND MILITIA 1689-1754	9
CHAPTER 1	*Contenders, 1689-1691*	11
CHAPTER 2	*Patterns of Colonial Conflict, 1692-1754*	37
PART TWO	GUERILLAS AND GRENADIERS 1755-1760	61
CHAPTER 3	*Battle Array, 1755*	63
CHAPTER 4	*Braddock's Offensive, 1755*	82
CHAPTER 5	*Vaudreuil's Offensive, 1756-1757*	97
CHAPTER 6	*Pitt's Offensive, 1758-1760*	111
Epilogue: Sugar or Snow		129
	Notes	135
	Bibliographical Note	144
	Index	150

Introduction

As the past is an approach to the present, it is not surprising that the struggle for Canada has been a war of pens ever since it ceased to be a war of swords. While partisans continue sniping, nationalists either emphasize the Canadian *vs.* American aspects of the struggle or spotlight the "mingling of blood" on the Plains of Abraham, with accolades of gallantry, honour and justice distributed to all. Michel Brunet has rightfully warned nationalistic historians:

> A true and fruitful partnership between French and English Canadians cannot be based upon a common misunderstanding of Canadian history and Canadian society.[1]

When does Canada begin? Only English-speaking Canadians have difficulty with this question, and they are not always aware of it. If Canada is a place, the answer is relatively easy. If Canada is a people, is the answer the same? Here is the crux, but the problem is not always apparent.

English-speaking Canadians usually manage to resolve the conflict, and stay in the winner's circle, with a little subconscious sleight of hand. If they are willing to identify with Champlain and Hébert, they share in twice as much Canadian history as they would if they confine themselves, vicariously, to the role of conquerors. If their sympathies are with the Canadian beginnings of 1604, where do they "cross the lines" to join the baggage train of the British generals, Amherst and Wolfe? Is Sir William Phips, leader of the New England assault on Quebec in 1690, seen as an unsuccessful liberator or as an American invader at whom Count Frontenac hurls defiance? Is William Pepperell, heir of the Phips tradition, appreciated for liberating Louisbourg in 1745, or seen as an invader who is more successful than Phips? In reading of the defeat of General Braddock at the Monongahela River in 1755, is the reader among the Indians and Canadians sharp-shooting from cover, or is he amid the chaos and despair of Braddock's men? Are sympathies with the winning Canadians at Oswego in 1756, Fort William Henry in 1757, and Fort Carillon in 1758 only to change as the inevitable happens elsewhere in 1758 and the two campaigns to come?

All of these choices are in the realm of half-realized sympathies, not historical realities, but the influence of these sympathies is unmistakable and is reinforced by the choice of weighted words used to describe the people involved. For instance, the term "French Canadian" can imply that the person is not totally Canadian, or that being a Canadian can mean being something other than being a French Canadian. In the period under discussion neither alternative is meaningful. Another term, "French and Indian", is most frequently used by American writers, and carries something of Cotton Mather's meaning:

> ... the French, with Indians, being Half one, half t'other, Half Indianized French, and Half Frenchified Indians.[2]

"French and Indian", in addition to the fact that it refers to Canada's two major sources of help rather than to the Canadians themselves, is not a phrase which encourages either sympathy or neutrality in many readers. "Canadian" is preferable, both for its accuracy and to emphasize the problem of loyalties. Perhaps this explanation of the use of the term "Canadian" will help to justify the use of the term "American", even if the coherent separate identity of the latter is more doubtful—at least with reference to the first years under discussion. This usage allows the terms "British" ("English" before the Act of Union with Scotland in 1707) to be applied more accurately.

One additional word needs explanation. The term "Indian" has even less meaning than that other collective, "white man". In military strength and effectiveness, in the economic basis of their societies, and in loyalties, the original possessors of all these battlefields provide incredible variety. Yet the accounts left by "white men" (and "white men" have a virtual monopoly of the surviving accounts) do not always suggest appreciation of, or interest in, many tribal differences. And how easy it must have been to depreciate the Indian contribution to victory, and enhance Indian responsibility for defeat, with a monopoly of history.

If something as limited as words of description is weighted heavily with interpretation, how crucial is the structure of an investigation of this subject? If the emphasis is put upon the "Seven Years' War in America", with what happened before considered as relatively unimportant, an author is automatically favouring the British at the expense of the Americans, the French and even the Canadians. Why? Because this is a British victory achieved in a relatively short period and achieved with uneven American support. Lawrence Henry Gipson's massive and important study, *The British Empire before the American Revolution*, which skilfully places the struggle for Canada in its global context, is the most important work of this kind. Concentration upon the Seven Years' War can serve another purpose, as best seen in Guy Frégault's *La Guerre de la Conquête*. Frégault considers the fall of New France largely in terms of the mistakes and self-interest of France and Frenchmen in the New World. The failure of France, like the victory of Britain, is particularly evident within the context of New France's last decade.[3]

What preconceptions are nurtured by viewing the struggle as a unit from 1689-1760? This larger canvas gives the struggle more heroic proportions. In the same way that cultural survival can be considered victory for French Canadians in modern Canada, so military survival can be viewed as victory in the eighteenth century. Seventy years of survival were seventy years of victory. Also, if defeat is seen coming from afar it is easier to consider it as inevitable. This absolves those who lose while limiting the credit given to those who win. Gustave Lanctôt writes:

> The conquest, which had been a threat ever since the expedition of Phipps three quarters of a century earlier (1690), may be attributed to three main causes: an inadequate population, hostility on the part of the English colonies and France's continental policy.[4]

Seen, then, as a tenacious and heroic struggle against the inevitable, the story of wars from 1689 to 1763 cannot help but attract French-Canadian writers.

Of course, the comprehensive view of the "Half Century of Conflict" or the "Second Hundred Years' War" is as popular in English as it is in French. If the differences between the British and the American colonists are minimized, the subject becomes a long, heroic and successful struggle fought and won by Anglo-American, or "Anglo-Saxon", effort. There is still room for the inevitability of the victory, in this interpretation, too. Amid patronizing admiration for the heroic losers, it is often possible to sense belief in the inherent superiority of the "Anglo-Saxon" or his institutions. Francis Parkman, the greatest narrator of this topic, revealed the prejudices of his own time when he wrote of the final struggle:

> It was the strife, too, of the past against the future; of the old against the new; of moral and intellectual torpor against moral and intellectual life; of barren absolutism against a liberty, crude, incoherent, and chaotic, yet full of prolific vitality.[5]

While few writers are as obvious in branding New France an enemy of progress, and thereby doomed and damned, some of this brand remains on much of English and American scholarship. One recent account is as explicit as Parkman. Howard H. Peckham, whose *The Colonial Wars 1689-1762* appeared in 1964, wrote on the same subject as Parkman's above statement:

> Subtly perhaps but definitely in this last war the Renaissance made its final conquest of a feudal mind.
>
> . . . .
>
> Only a few individuals, like Champlain or La Salle or Frontenac, who broke from the feudal mold possessed the liberal faith or broad patriotism to envision a French empire of mutually supporting parts. . . . New France, actually a misnomer, was truly an extension of the Old World, and therein lay its failing.[6]

Obviously, the concept of inevitability has its advantages for both sides. The broader picture is as popular in the American context as it is in the French-Canadian. Before the historian's pen is put to paper, his view of who and what his subject is, affects what his answers will be.

Admitting that any form of inquiry will, and should, emphasize some theme, what preconceptions are implied in the structuring of this essay? The story is divided into two major parts, representing those contests dominated by the colonists (1689-1754) and the final struggle which was controlled largely by Europeans (1755-1760). The longer and more heroic account is given a place without diluting the importance of the relatively short and decisive climax.

The organization of this inquiry also tends to sharpen the contrasts between decidedly different types of warfare: guerilla war, and warfare according to European convention. The term "guerilla" war is used here in a general sense, to mean an offensive by small groups of men able to "live off the land", strike hard at vital and vulnerable targets, enhance the impact of small raids by terrifying brutality, then melt into the countryside before they could be counterattacked. In such circumstances bravery and honour were measured by different standards from those of Europe. The brave were those who won and lived, or who died defiant at a stake in some enemy's camp. This prototype of present-day guerilla war was the war of the North American Indian. His bow was silent, gave off no flash of light or puff of smoke, was usable in wet weather, and was at least as accurate as most seventeenth century muskets. The supporting arms, the hatchet and the knife, were also well-suited for surprise raids. The Indian's weapons probably helped form his type of war, a type particularly useful in paralyzing superior numbers of white settlers.

Europeans who migrated to North America had suffered from the limitations of the flintlock musket, but they soon disposed of the matchlock and pike they had brought with them, and began to carry knives and even hatchets.[7] By 1750 the longer, lighter, more accurate Pennsylvania or Kentucky rifle was common among American frontiersmen, though not in the American militias. The Pennsylvania rifle was neither silent nor easy to handle in wooded country, but it was accurate. It would not carry a bayonet, but its owner was usually

Introduction ❖ 5

unwilling to stand on an unprotected firing line to deliver or receive a bayonet charge in any event. Adaptation to the warfare practised by the Indians was vital to survival for the first white settlers in the New World. Even after colonies were firmly established, men who lived on the fringes of settlement maintained a familiarity with the prototype of guerilla war.

Conventional warfare was carried to the New World again during the Seven Years' War, this time by large numbers of European troops. It can be said that they influenced this war more than it influenced them. European war in the middle of the eighteenth century was formal, professional and mercenary. Kings hired armies to fight, not for religious principles nor patriotism, but to settle dynastic controversies. Officers led for honour, soldiers fought for a living. Most of the peasants, artisans, and traders lived and worked as usual, although they were keenly interested in the outcome of the war games and were taxed to pay for them. Civilians were safer in these wars than in the religious wars before or the national wars to follow; the kings who hired troops had to supply them, rather than permit the earlier savagery of "living off the land". Supply depots were like stakes to which armies were chained, limiting offensive operations. Armies were a royal investment, and trained armies were not to be squandered in battles that won nothing but "the day". As Daniel Defoe remarked:

> The present maxims of war are—Never fight without a manifest advantage, and always encamp so as not to be forced to it. And if two opposite generals nicely observe both these rules, it is impossible they should ever come to fight.... This way of making war spends generally more money and less blood than former wars did.[8]

Battles occurred, nonetheless, and could be very bloody. The ideal site was an open, level area flanked by geographic allies like marshes, cliffs, or rivers. Here the opposing forces met as parallel ranks of three or four men marching in close order. Firing was by volley, for individual weapons were unreliable. One rank fired while the other two or three were reloading. This line of fire was expected to stand and defend itself against a bayonet charge, while cavalry charges were met with cavalry, and all were supported by field cannon.

Yet, even if won, murderous battles were not the main strategic objective of war. The peace treaty was the goal of the war in a real sense, the fighting was to obtain a favourable settlement of dispute, not to destroy a religion or an ideology. Since possession of a fortress was tantamount to holding the surrounding territory, a major strategic object was to take and hold fortresses. These could later be used for bargaining in negotiations. Sieges were a common form of offensive and their conduct was circumscribed by conventions. The commander defending a fortress could not surrender prematurely on pain of court martial, nor too late as the besiegers would then slaughter the garrison and loot the town. If the walls had been breached by enemy cannon fire, after the enemy trenches which had started 600 yards from the walls had zigzagged their way to within 100 yards, the defenders were not expected to withstand more than one assault upon the breach. The garrison would be allowed to leave, armed, carrying their standards, and accompanied by martial music. They might also be required to desist fighting for a year. Prisoners of war, or hostages, were to be cared for and exchanged or returned as soon as possible.

Mixing two types of war as vastly different as those suggested here created a very explosive brew. Either type of war was terrifying enough, but not knowing which one was being used must have been horrifying. A commander of a besieged frontier fortress might presume that unless conventional rules were being applied there would be no siege. But unruly guerillas might violate the "laws of war" after surrender. Colonists who were not familiar with frontier life, and who outnumbered their opponents markedly, would favour an adapted version of conventional warfare. The co-operation, confusion and contest between these types of warfare is a theme emphasized by the organization of this book.

Even if themes are served by the structuring of this study, the themes are not the primary purpose. The main objective is to invite thoughtful consideration of some aspects of a large, diffuse, and important subject. The questioning of answers is, and must be, at least as important as the answering of questions.

PART ONE

FRONTIERSMEN AND MILITIA
1689-1754

Chapter 1

Contenders, 1689-1691

The North American version of the War of the League of Augsburg (1689-1697), most inappropriately titled King William's War by the Americans, officially opened a seventy-year struggle for the continent. North American military resources, methods, and objectives dominated the first three of the four wars in this long duel: the War of the League of Augsburg, the War of the Spanish Succession (1702-1713), and the War of the Austrian Succession (1744-1748). Much of the story of the colonial aspects of these three wars can be seen as variations on themes apparent in the first three years of the fighting. Analysis of the goals, strengths, and weaknesses of the various contenders in 1689, as made apparent by the military action of the first three years, should help to explain why this phase of the contest was as long, as intermittent, and as indecisive as it proved to be.

EUROPEAN CONTENDERS

England and France did not fight in or for North America for years after 1689. To these European powers the North American theatre was an insignificant sideshow to a much more important and expensive European main event. For example, the highlight of the North American fighting in the eventful year of 1704 was a raid by 340 Canadians and Indians upon Deerfield, Massachusetts, causing the death of 65 persons; however, in and around the little Danube town of Blenheim on a single day that summer more than 100,000 men fought, and nearly half of them died.

The Duke of Marlborough, in charge of England's troops

throughout most of the War of the Spanish Succession, disliked sending expeditions to the colonies:

> I dare not speak against the project of sending troops to the West Indies, the Cabinet Council thinking it very reasonable. But to you I will own very freely that I think it can end in nothing but a great expence and the ruining of those regiments. Besides, nothing that can be done there will forward the peace; and if we can be so fortunate as to force them here, we may have by one dash of a pen much more than any expeditions can give in many years.[1]

England and France were preoccupied with their larger struggle, thereby isolating the North American theatre and making it a contest *by* colonists and *for* colonists.

Yet there were two times in each war when this policy was not so evident. At the time of both declarations of war there was a race, focusing on the more valuable West Indian possessions, to bring news of war to the colonies and to bring a hastily-raised invasion to enemy islands. An English raid on Guadeloupe in 1691 was a much-delayed venture of this sort. The other time at which the colonies loomed larger than usual in European minds was during the negotiations for peace. Fighting in the distant colonies would not seriously jeopardize negotiations and might well yield something of enough value to alter the complexion of the peace settlement. During the Ryswick negotiations (1697) an English representative complained that the French were delaying in order to await the outcome of their raid on Cartagena.[2] The Walker expedition of 1711 (see below, pp. 39-40) can also be seen in this larger context of peace negotiation. Both the approach of war and the approach of peace gave the colonial struggle some measure of significance, though no priority in the minds of European strategists.

A seaborne empire, gained and kept by men-of-war, was more vital to England and more valuable to France than the struggle for the scalps of men and the skins of beaver. Sea power meant trade; trade meant wealth; wealth meant power. Jean Colbert made France aware of this, and spared no effort as Minister of Marine to convince Louis XIV that a powerful fleet was necessary for the maintenance and improvement of the King's position. The miraculous result was that, in 1689, France had the largest navy in Europe, built up under Colbert from 20 ships in 1661 to over 250 by 1677—a fleet capable of matching the combined Anglo-Dutch navies.[3] Sharpened by frequent skirmishes with Barbary pirates, this instrument was powerful, if somewhat brittle in comparison with that of its opponents. The Dutch and English reserve of seamen was larger, and proximity to the Baltic sources of timber, pitch, tar, and hemp meant that refitting ships would be easier for the Dutch and English, and harder for the French. What is more, Colbert died more than five years before the great struggle began; the French victory at Beachy Head in July 1690 was his posthumous success. But the French navy lost more than a battle in May 1692 at La Hogue—it also lost the favour of King Louis XIV. After 1693 the French fleet, as such, did not contest the command of the sea. Thereafter, the French war at sea was almost wholly entrusted to a generation of able and courageous privateers, including Jean Bart, Réné Duguay-Trouin, and Pierre le Moyne d'Iberville. Their highly successful operations were of the same nature as those of the Elizabethan sea-dogs—they could "singe the beard" of the opponent, distracting but not defeating him.

But all of this was still to come in 1689, when France had the largest fleet in Europe, and the best army. Communications with colonies were not as yet interrupted by "command of the sea" by either England or France. The aid sent was very limited, but not as yet limited by one power's preponderance at sea.

CANADA (NEW FRANCE)

It seems incredible that it could take seventy years to settle the military contest between Canada and her English-speaking neighbours to the south, since the population figures for 1689 suggested odds of nearly twenty to one against the Canadians.[4] While the answer to this puzzle is almost wholly a discussion of why the English colonies did not win an early victory, it is also important to consider some of the reasons why the Canadians did not lose.

Though the political leadership of New France in 1689 left

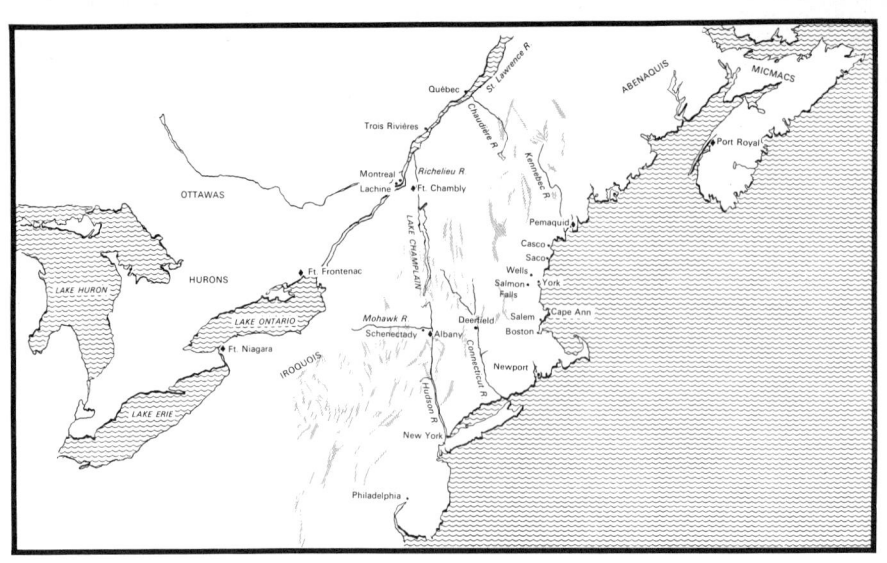

THE CANADIAN-AMERICAN FRONTIER, 1689

something to be desired, there was real strength in the unified political power which left the governor subject only to annual review in Paris on an *ex post facto* basis. The incessant squabbles among governor, intendant, and bishop cannot obliterate the fact that marshalling of resources, negotiating with Indians, and planning strategy were all greatly facilitated by the unity of the colony. Though Canada's boundaries were not defined, in 1689 the governor of New France had diplomatic and military authority as the King's representative in all French-held and French-claimed territory in North America. Acadia's position was ambiguous, but it was clear that in wartime the governor of New France was commander there as well.*

Though every year that New France survived against her colossal opponents could be considered a year of victory, some English-speaking historians persist in viewing Canadian society as inherently feeble. Professor Howard H. Peckham, of the University of Michigan, writes:

> France had clung too long to outworn concepts of the Middle Ages. She represented a closed society under four authorities: monarch, church, nobility, and monopoly. She secured obedience and uniformity in New France at the expense of initiative and self-reliance.[5]

*By 1701 the small French settlement of Plaisance, Newfoundland, was not subject to Quebec City, nor was the new colony of Louisiana.

14 ❖ *Guerillas and Grenadiers*

But the role of all four authorities must be qualified upon closer scrutiny of the administration of New France and of the impact of the fur trade on Canadian life. If a seventeenth-century monarch provided authoritarian and paternalistic government which did not tax colonists and was relatively efficient, honest, and just, did he do his duty to his colonial subjects?[6] Did the life of adventure and freedom associated with the fur trade foster initiative and self-reliance at the expense of the power of the Church and the manor house?[7] The luxury trade in furs helped build the fortunes of a monied group of Canadians, whose apparent absence has been lamented by many earlier historians.[8] Increasingly, the historian's picture of Canadian society before 1760 is being made more compatible with the obvious initiative, resilience, and persistence of those three generations which fought for a continent.

In seeking to explain the military success and failure of New France, understandable emphasis has been placed on the condition of her economy. In reply to those who claim that initiative was squashed by government control, W. J. Eccles, of the University of Toronto, argues:

> . . . it was not state paternalism that stifled economic development, or initiative, in New France, but its sudden cessation [after 1672].[9]

Whether less government control or more government investment in new industries might have helped, the fact remains that, by 1689, the economy of New France was not diversified. The fur trade was by far the most important source of capital, and this trade was especially vulnerable in wartime, when bringing the furs from up-country was precarious, and the sea passage became less secure. By the end of the first Anglo-French war in America there was enough fur stockpiled in Canadian warehouses to supply the whole European market for more than a decade.[10] Agriculture was also unusually vulnerable to the disruption of war. New France did not have much surplus in good years like 1689, and there was real hardship caused by poor crops in 1687 and 1690.[11] War meant that men would be fighting instead of sowing or reaping, that additional recruits sent from France—though welcome—would be a serious drain

Contenders, 1689-1691 ❖ 15

on limited grain supplies, and that farming in the dispersed settlements along the St. Lawrence would be a dangerous pursuit. War made New France more dependent on shipments of French food, war materials and manufactures, yet the sea lanes were vulnerable and French government help uncertain. Canadians could not afford long wars—or even long campaigns.

A muster of the military strength of Canada can be taken from the largest offensive raid made by the Canadians in the first generation of the duel—Denonville's attack on the Senecas in June 1687—before the war with England's colonies had formally begun. Gathered at Montreal were 900 Canadian militiamen. (It was never difficult to gather militia volunteers for the guerilla raids in subsequent years.) The force also included 832 *troupes de la marine** and 400 Indian allies from around Montreal. As this army approached Seneca country it was joined by the Ottawas, from the west, and the *coureurs de bois*.[13] The total striking force approached 3,000 fighting men. By 1689, another 1,100 *troupes de la marine* had been sent to the colony. Even with a reduction in number due to disease and casualties, Canada had nearly 1,000 militiamen and 1,500 *troupes de la marine* as well as a fluctuating number of Indian allies to defend her.

Nature herself helped with the defense of Canada. The northern reaches of the Appalachians—the Green Mountains of Vermont, and the White Mountains of New Hampshire and Maine—as well as the Adirondacks of New York, effectively protected much of Canada's frontier from her more populous neighbours. These defenses had three gates, the St. Lawrence itself, the Hudson-Lake Champlain-Richelieu waterway, and the Lake Ontario-upper St. Lawrence approach. All these gates were narrow enough to be commanded, in a European sense, by forts. In the case of the St. Lawrence, Quebec City was both a gate and a citadel. In neither of the other cases was there anything as effective in 1689. The forts on the Richelieu River, while they hindered use of that waterway, could not stop raids

---

*These were not French regulars, but French-recruited independent companies. There were no regular French soldiers in Canada between 1668, when most of the Carignan-Salières Regiment returned to France, and 1755.[12]

overland from the northern end of Lake Champlain. Later fortifications at the southern end of the lake could and did block this route. The Lake Ontario-upper St. Lawrence approach could not be closed to canoes by a fort, though extensive rapids flanked by forts were barriers to European transports seventy years later.

When, in 1688, the governor of New France decided to demolish Fort Frontenac because it could not be supplied safely, he was making a sound military move. The defencelessness of this western gateway was made horrifyingly clear the following year when the Iroquois attacked at Lachine. But the Iroquois were not lackeys of New York, and vacillated between alliance with these Americans and, increasingly, a more practical neutrality. Even without the interposition of these proud and suspicious people, New Yorkers would have found the western route a toilsome 350 miles from their frontier settlement at Schenectady, compared with 200 miles by the Lake Champlain route. So, in this first generation of war, the Canadians' most vulnerable front involved the Iroquois alone. American or British assaults took the form of two-pronged attacks, an armada in the St. Lawrence and a land invasion up the Hudson-Lake Champlain-Richelieu route.

The least defensible gate into the heart of New France was the important gateway for Canadian expansion into the interior of the continent. The fight for fur between the Canadians and the Iroquois was a murderous sort of leap-frog which did more to promote Canadian explorations than did the lure of the fabulous waterways themselves. By 1689 the Canadians had won the fight for the Illinois country and beyond.[14] In the eighteenth century this contest would become an integral part of the Anglo-French struggle. In 1689, however, it could still be viewed as distinct. The west was a place where hundreds of Canadians fought with Huron and Ottawa allies against Iroquois enemies for the high stakes of the fur trade. The war for the west was a training in guerilla warfare that created a cadre of tough and versatile, if savage and poorly-disciplined, raiders. These rugged "Indianized-French" would bring their talents to the Canadian-American struggle. They led tortuous winter marches to do the brutal work at Schenectady, Salmon Falls,

Casco and Deerfield. They matched the ferocity and success of the Iroquois destruction at Lachine.

The Hudson-Lake Champlain-Richelieu route was an invitation to apply the ways of war learned in the west. When a raiding party set out up the Richelieu their destination could be anywhere from Schenectady to Casco, 200 miles apart. With a minimum of warning, the frontier settlements of Maine, New Hampshire, Massachusetts, or New York might suffer a demonic visitation. Any land invasion from the American colonists, by contrast, would be forced to funnel into the Lake Champlain-Richelieu River route. Even if entry by this route could not be blocked by the Canadians, surprise was minimized and the American retreat could be made very difficult. There was only one way in which nature was unkind toward the defences of Canada. On both the St. Lawrence, which contributed so much to the mobility of the Canadians, and the Hudson-Lake Champlain-Richelieu waterways, there were several weeks between the breakup of ice for American forces moving northward and the clearing of the ice from the waters flowing through the heart of New France, which permitted Canadian movement south and west from Montreal. This American advantage of water transportation earlier in the spring and later in the autumn was to become a more important military factor during the last phase of the struggle, when relatively small and self-sufficient raiding parties were replaced by larger armies even more dependent on water routes for transport and supplies. Except for this inherent weakness, the geography of Canada was a valuable ally for the Canadians.

Acadia was an isolated settlement beyond these geographic outworks, lame in defence, but the base of operations for a mighty guerilla offensive against New England. A few privateers working out of Port Royal harassed Boston's trade. But these were of little consequence when compared to the Abenaquis war upon the New Englanders of Maine. With plenty of encouragement and relatively little practical help, Canada was able to keep the military resources of Massachusetts, including its only brilliant guerila leader, Benjamin Church, busy for much of the generation after 1689. The weakness of Acadia, however, was made very clear by the capture of Port Royal in

1690, in which 700 men obtained a surrender from a garrison of sixty-five men with only forty firearms among them.[15]

Indians were not only tutors to the Canadians in the forest wars, but also very important allies. From Champlain's time, the Canadians had joined the Algonquin peoples and the Hurons against their Iroquois kin. This was a dangerous choice of allies for the Canadians, but one demanded by the fur trade economy of Canada. As the war with the American colonies approached, the Canadians had an impressive array of allies—the Abenaquis of modern New Brunswick, the Ottawas and subsidiary Algonquin peoples, and the Hurons. In the 1680's the Canadians had confirmed their links with the Miami tribe (between the Ohio River and Lake Michigan), and had won the struggle for the trade of the Illinois (west of the Miami to the Mississippi River). These two tribes added 3,000 potential warriors to the Canadian side, though they were too far west to be used in anything but defensive action against the Iroquois.[16] Moreover, these Miami and Illinois allies were understandably suspicious of the Canadian traders. The approach of the Canadians meant that a tribe could, for a time, serve as middlemen in trade with more distant tribes, and enjoy the important advantage of European weapons. But the Canadian *coureurs de bois* could be expected to penetrate deeper into the west one day, for they did not appreciate extra middlemen. Yet the Canadians had proved more successful than the Iroquois in mixing threats and concessions to gain allies in the west. On the northern New England frontier, against the persistent, land-hungry *Bastonnais*, the Canadians could pose as defenders of the Indian way of life in 1689. In their contact with the Indians, the Canadians were usually interested in furs, not farms, and hence in the preservation of the Indian life of hunting and trapping. By the middle of the eighteenth century, when the Iroquois no longer served as a buffer between the Americans and the tribes of the interior, the Canadians could use the same argument to a much wider audience. (See below, pp. 66-68.)

Canada's advantages and resources, as well as her limitations, determined the type of war that could, and would, be undertaken. As the struggle with the Americans began, Iroquois raids reached a climax with a 1,500-man attack on Lachine. Then all was mercifully quiet. In 1689, the elusive but ever-present Iroquois war parties had given the Canadians yet another fierce demonstration of how a numerically inferior martial group could inflict paralysis on a more powerful neighbour. The Canadians would apply a similar strategy in order to utilize the advantages of political unity and geographic defenses, as well as the experience the allies derived from the fur trade. Guerilla warfare also lessened the effects of Canada's inferiority in manpower and resources.

THE AMERICAN COLONIES

Canadians quaked at the sight of an American invasion in 1690; yet this challenge did not come close to representing the full strength of the colonies on the American seaboard. The potential strength of 200,000 American colonists was irrelevant in this contest. In reality, 10,000 Canadians were fighting 48,000 *Bastonnais* and 20,000 New Yorkers, plus the 20,000 people of Connecticut who were engaged only intermittently in active hostility. There was an imbalance of numbers, but not as great as might be supposed.

Derision has been heaped upon the American colonists for their parochialism in being unwilling to co-operate and drive out the Canadians, but the charge is heavily weighted with hindsight. In view of the momentous differences in origin, religion, and the stage of development, disunity in English America should be a presumption, not an accusation. In 1689 the American colonists were not dreaming of that unity which would become reality for their grandsons. Land and commerce, the economic basis of colonial life, brought competition and conflict to the beginnings of intercolonial relations—more friction, indeed, than with the far-off Canadians. Most of English America was not threatened by, and not interested in, New France. For example, with or without Quaker scruples about war, Pennsylvania would lose much more than she would gain by participating in the war to the north. A colony less than a decade old, defending itself primarily with an enlightened Indian policy, Pennsylvania would be courting disaster by involving itself in a war far enough away to exclude gains, yet close enough to risk bringing war to her own frontier. A Virginian displayed a similar lack of interest when he later complained:

> I know during the late War, the *New York* Men made a great noise, that they defended all our Frontiers, and therefore ought in reason to be assisted by the Neighbouring Colonies, but the truth of the matter was, they only defended themselves and their own Trade with the *Indians*.[17]

There was also little reason for concern in the Carolinas. It was a frontier area in 1689, sharing a border with England's ally, Spain. As yet the French challenge had not come to the southern frontier; even when it did, it actually reinforced the lack of interest in the problems of the north. This struggle at the south end of the Appalachians would have few links with the war to the north. The Carolinas, Virginia, Maryland, and Pennsylvania were still quite safe behind the Appalachians—ramparts in 1689 rather than barriers. The Jerseys, Rhode Island, and even Connecticut, were screened from the war by the colonies of New York and Massachusetts. American colonists did not display apathy and self-interest to any unusual degree. The fate of the grand designs against Canada seemed to justify the colonist who had decided to defend his home, his town, or his colony, rather than England's empire in America.

Colonial unity was very improbable; English policy in the three years before 1689 had made it all but impossible. James II and his advisers had shown a sound grasp of the larger problems of the empire in America, but in surveying the woods they did not notice any of the trees. While they could see a united Dominion of New England as an overwhelming counterweight to Canada, they could not, or would not, see the animosity which the imposed solution would engender. In 1686 Massachusetts (including Maine), New Hampshire, Connecticut, and Rhode Island were united administratively under a single royal governor. By 1688 this government was extended south to the borders of Pennsylvania. Nearly 110,000 people were then under a single government based at Boston. Among the colonists this co-operation, enforced by royal decree (for representative institutions were suppressed) was called tyranny. Pious men of Massachusetts prayed that their former liberties might be restored:

> We know not indeed what God may unexpectedly do for us if we sit still either by sudden turning the heart of the King to favor us, or other ways providentially diverting what is intended & resolved concerning us....[18]

When the miracle came, in the form of the successful invasion of England by William of Orange, and the flight and deposition of James II, men of New England scrambled for past liberties and new assurances. The English revolution of 1688 was staged in miniature in Boston and New York.

As the first war with New France began, turmoil existed in those English colonies that would have to bear most of the burden of the struggle. It was not an auspicious beginning, as one English official, writing from jail in Boston to the authorities in England, lamented:

> The French have above four thousand good men about Canada, ready for any designe. I expect that upon the newes of the Bostoners reassuming their old government (no care being taken for the out-towns and Provinces) they will joyne with the Indians, and in a short time swallow and be master of that part of the Countrey . . . and then being possessed of our best ports & harbours, be masters of all the great masts in New England and will infest the trade of other [of] the English forraine plantacôns; the prevention whereof was one chiefe ground of putting all those petty governments under one generall Governour.[19]

There was little optimism about the collective strength of the American colonies to resist and defeat Canada; the colonists did not think collectively. There was even less cause for optimism when individual colonies were considered, especially those forced into the struggle immediately—Massachusetts and New York.

Massachusetts. Wealth and power had aided Massachusetts in winning many boundary disputes with her neighbours. Perhaps it was only right that, as a result, the Massachusetts General Court was responsible for defending more than 200 miles of frontier against the Canadians. However, 1689 was no year for reinforcing the frontiers with the able-bodied men of this colony of some 50,000 souls. Even the 500 men who had been stationed on the eastern frontier in 1688 were not there by the summer of 1689. Some had been recalled to maintain order in Boston, others carried out their own petty revolts, seizing officers and going home. Indian fury would fill the vacuum created. Chaos, not cowardice, caused this colony—with five times the population of Canada, and more than five times its wealth—to retreat so easily from what was just the beginning of the offensive on the eastern frontier.

Geography was worse than neutral to Massachusetts. The advantages that the Lake Champlain waterway provided the Canadians could not be used against them. (See above, p. 18.) Massachusetts settlements on the upper Connecticut River were more difficult to defend from Boston than they would have been from Connecticut, whose 20,000 people lived down-river from the pioneers at Deerfield, Northampton, Westfield, and Springfield, Massachusetts. The raw and vulnerable Maine frontier was separated from Boston by the weak and sparsely-settled colony of New Hampshire. Almost all communications between Maine and Boston would be by sea in any case, but the dubious insulation that New Hampshire provided against Indian attack upon Massachusetts proper did not help the war effort. Nature gave Massachusetts the admirably defensible harbour at Boston, and war gave Boston the opportunity to increase its hold on the shipping industry of Massachusetts, at the expense of more exposed minor ports such as Salem and Cape Ann. The sea was worth a great deal more to Massachusetts than it cost, but war made the mixed nature of the blessing readily apparent. While privateering against French and Canadian vessels was profitable and popular, war was particularly hard on the smaller vessels and the smaller seaports—in both cases they were inadequately equipped for defence. By land and sea Massachusetts was particularly vulnerable to demoralizing surprise attacks by Canadian and Algonquin raiders from the west, by Abenaquis raiders from the north and east, and by Canadian, West Indian, or French privateers on the coast.

Collapse of royal government, signalled by the imprisonment of the governor and rejection of the Dominion of New England less than a month before war was declared between England and France, meant that Massachusetts could not be ready to fight. The provisional government, headed by Simon Bradstreet, could not raise taxes for defence, or call for a levy of men. Bradstreet endeavoured to vindicate the government's efforts, but was forced to admit to the English authorities:

> The Indian war we have endeavoured to check, but ineffectually, by seeking out the provoking causes, but our efforts have been of no avail. The Indians, doubtless incited by the French, continued their hostility, increasing their numbers until we were obliged to levy soldiers to repel them. They have made great depredations in New Hampshire and Maine and some in Massachusetts, but Maine is the chief seat of war. A considerable force is already abroad against them in two bodies to the eastward by the joint concurrence of ourselves, Connecticut and New Plymouth, but the woods and rivers make it difficult to come up with the enemy, it being their manner to skulk or move in small parties. It is for God to give us success, though our efforts for defence have not been wholly unsuccessful. The whole expense has been borne by a few private persons, there being no public Treasury to be found upon the Revolution and the stores of ammunition being very low. We hope that what we have done may not be judged offensive. We cannot think ourselves secure from the French, who are said to be in great force in the West Indies. Pray assure their Majesties. . . .[20]

While the Puritan provisional government wrestled with defence, Puritanism relied on its own defence. As Cotton Mather later noted:

> It is remarkable to see that when the Unchurched Villages have been so many of them, *utterly broken up*, in the *War*, that has been upon us, those that have had *Churches* regularly formed in them, have generally been under a more *sensible Protection* of Heaven.[21]

Mather saw the war against evil spirits climaxing in the famous Salem witch trials of 1692, as related to the war against the Canadians and their Indian allies.

> The Story of the Prodigious War, made by the Spirits of the Invisible World upon the People of New-England, in the year, 1692, hath Entertain'd a great part of the English world, with a just Astonishment: and I have met with some Strange Things, not here to be mentioned, which have made me often think, that this inexplicable War might have some of its Original [origin] among the Indians, whose chief Sagamores are well known unto some of our Captives, to have been horrid Sorcerers, and hellish Conjurers and such as Conversed with Daemons.[22]

Indian allies played a much smaller part in the defence of Massachusetts than in the defence of Canada or of New York. Much of the difference can be seen as a result of Massachusetts' fiercest Indian war, King Philip's War (1675 to 1676). Many scars remained from this war when Massachusetts began her fight with the Canadians and confidence in racial harmony was shattered as a result. Approximately 5,000 Indians had been killed before the two-year struggle ended, and several tribes had been virtually annihilated. Massachusetts had had a weak Indian shield against New France in any case, and after King Philip's War, death, confusion, disillusion and migration had made it appreciably weaker. The French-allied Abenaquis had already gained a reputation as the Iroquois of the eastern seaboard, the fierce hunters who could terrorize the Indian farmers south of the Kennebec River. King Philip's War had made their task easier. Certainly no one in New France would have listed "... securing and disarming of Neighbouring *Indians* ..." among the "... things necessary for the safety of the out Plantations and the Prosecution and Suppression of the Enemy, ..." as did the Boston authorities in the spring of 1689.[23] Massachusetts had destroyed the Indian buffer, which might have limited the effect and the success of Canadian raids.

It might be thought that King Philip's War would have been an initiation into woodland warfare, which would have aided the *Bastonnais* immensely in the forthcoming struggle with the

Canadians. It is true that Benjamin Church made his reputation as a warrior in 1675 and 1676, and then le^d five expeditions against the Abenaquis in King William's War. Yet Church's methods were not at all common among the men who fought for Massachusetts after 1689. During a 1690 expedition he pleaded in vain with his men, American and Indian, that they should not light fires, as it would bring the Abenaquis down upon them. He was taunted as being afraid, but on the same night he was proven right.[24] Church shared the Indian aversion to forts, telling the unappreciative Sir William Phips that they were "only nests for destruction."[25] On the eve of war nearly half of New England's total strength of 13,279 men came from Massachusetts' seven regiments of foot and twelve troops of horse, organized and trained with a battlefield in mind.[26] In 1689 Massachusetts did not place Benjamin Church in charge of a rugged, irregular army of sharpshooting frontiersmen. The colony prepared European militia, led by the inexperienced Sir William Phips and determined to conquer the "citadels" of Port Royal and Quebec. Is it really surprising that this was New England's answer to the frontier raids of the Canadians or Abenaquis? Not at all. New France could answer the Iroquois in kind; New York could answer Canada in kind; New England tried to defend itself with search parties, frontier forts, bounties on raising mastiffs, or £100 bounties on Indian scalps,[27] but ultimately was forced to put its hope in a more ambitious and more dramatic invasion of Canada.

The hero of New England in 1689 was not the Indian fighter, but Sir William Phips. One of twenty-six children of a gunsmith with land on the Maine frontier, William Phips' good fortune began when he was a young ship's carpenter in Boston, where he met and married a wealthy widow. Luck enabled him to salvage a fortune from a sunken Spanish treasure galleon in the Caribbean, and thereby to obtain a knighthood as well as a modest portion of the £300,000 discovery. "The great adventurer, half crusader and half clown . . ."[28] led the two most significant Massachusetts offensives of the war, the attack on Port Royal and the siege of Quebec, both in 1690.

Attacking Port Royal and besieging Quebec were parts of

the same strategy. Cotton Mather explained this with a parable about chasing off rooks by cutting down the trees they nest in:

> The Indian Rooks grievously infested the Country; and while the Country was only on the Defensive Part, their Men were Thinned, their Towns were Broken, and their Treasure consumed, without any Hope of seeing an End of these Troublesome Tragedies. The French Colonies to the Northward were the Tree in which those Rooks had their Nests; and the French having in person first fallen upon the English of New-England, it was thought that the New-Englanders might very justly take this Occasion to Reduce those French Colonies under the English Government, and so at once take away from all the Rooks for ever, all that gave 'em any Advantage to Infest us.[29]

To continue Mather's metaphor, if the rooks cannot be shot, caught, or frightened away, and if something must be done, why not try to cut down the tree?

As Massachusetts legates prepared for the opening of an intercolonial conference which would plan an invasion of Canada, Sir William Phips set sail, early in May of 1690, with a force of 700 men bound for Port Royal. The troops, two-thirds of whom were conscripts, landed without opposition and challenged the fort. The Acadian governor, realizing that his decrepit fort had only a tenth of the manpower and none of the firepower of the invaders, agreed to surrender*. A fort was taken, prisoners were taken, and a Massachusetts garrison replaced the French. Aside from pillaging, contrary to the articles of surrender, the successful excursion was conducted according to the rules and goals of European warfare. Taking the fort was only a gesture, for this pathetic little post which Phips demolished had not been a refuge for Abenaqui raiders and was not vital to privateers either.

Phips had been away from Boston for a month, and on his return was given command of a naval expedition that constituted the main force of an intercolonial invasion of Canada. Massachusetts had lost £3,000 in the conquest of Port Royal, and the provisional government was particularly hard-pressed

*See above, pp. 18-19. The fort's eighteen cannon were not mounted.

to outfit this second expedition. The English government had been asked for aid, but none arrived, although the colonists waited until well past midsummer. Reluctant Boston merchants were finally induced to invest in the venture. The resulting little armada might have been large enough if its timing, and that of the overland party from New York, had been perfect. Twenty-three hundred men, with supplies for three months, were put aboard thirty-two vessels, the largest of which would have been too small to sail in any European line of battle.[30]

Luck was not always with Phips on this expedition; it took two months to reach Quebec. Repeated landings to claim deserted stretches of the south shore of the Gulf of St. Lawrence were probably an impatient man's effort to busy himself while the fleet bucked headwinds or the sails hung limply.[31] Delay meant that smallpox was devouring more men, and the men were devouring more provisions. The most fortunate thing that happened to Phips (and the fate of the Walker expedition of 1711 showed that it was simply luck) was that the fleet, without experienced pilots, navigated the treacherous St. Lawrence without mishap. Phips may not have felt lucky as he gazed up at Quebec from the deck of the *Six Friends* on October 5 (October 16 by the modern calendar). He knew the overland expedition had failed to divert any of the estimated 3,000 defenders of the citadel. He knew smallpox was sweeping through his ranks. He knew the easterly winds that had finally let him sail to Quebec would make the trip home even more arduous and hungry, for two-thirds of the provisions were already consumed. And he knew ice already covered the streams at night, ice that could soon trap his ships and crush them like peapods in a vise.

Assaulting Quebec was the particular responsibility of 1,300 men, under one Major Walley, who landed three miles below Quebec on October 7. "... Ammunition, provision, field pieces, shovels, spades, and other necessarys for the souldiers, ..."[32] were to be landed by small armed craft. Bombardment of the citadel was to serve as a diversion and, as the main force advanced on the right flank, 200 men would be landed to scale the walls. The cannonade, directed by Phips, did little damage to Quebec although it consumed almost all of the powder in the

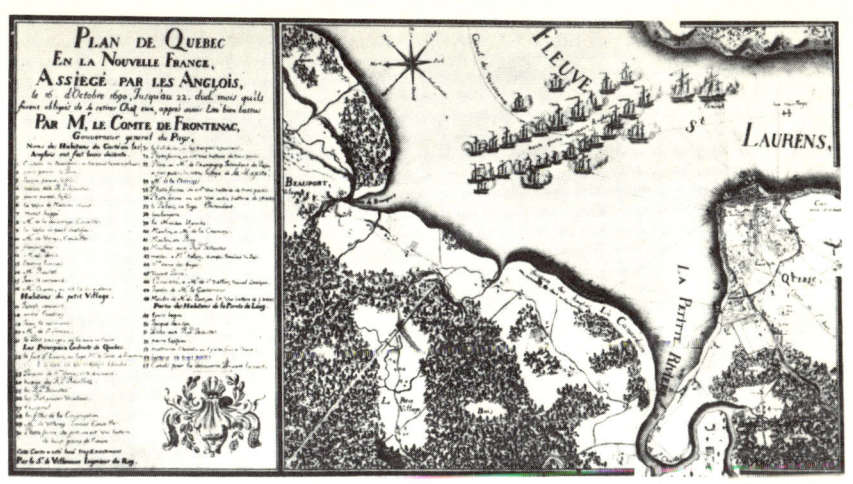

Phips at Quebec in 1690. This portrayal over-estimates the fleet, envisaging thirty-four three-masted vessels all firing mounted guns.

fleet and provoked a heavy answering fire that battered the vessels taking part in the attack. Also, ". . . the admiral being, as they say, forced to leave their best cable and anchor behind him and get back again,"[33] the failure meant that Phips was nearly as ready as his lieutenants to accept the conclusion that the mission would not succeed. Daniel Neale, fellow-colonist and historian of New England, assessed the causes of failure:

> The French confess, that there was no want of Bravery in the Soldiers, but impute their ill Success to their Unacquaintedness with Military Discipline, to their being enfeebled by the Fatigues of the Sea, and the ill Conduct of Sir *William Phips,* who upon this Enterprize could not have done the *French* a greater Service, if he had been hir'd to stand still with his hands in his Pocket.[34]

A twentieth-century New Englander, J. T. Adams, went further:

> The land forces under Walley had behaved well, but in re-embarking lost all semblance of discipline, took to the boats much like a base-ball crowd to the street cars, ... The self-flattering belief . . . that training of any sort is a waste of time, and that, in military affairs, competent commanders and disciplined troops can be found at any moment in a crisis, had again proved a costly fallacy.[35]

Contenders, 1689-1691 ❖ 29

Major Walley's journal, which is the best account of the assault from the attacking side, certainly supports this version of the re-embarkation:

> ... I ordered some souldiers to keep the rest from crowding down until those were gone off that were upon the flats; I called to them to be silent, but either of these were little regarded, for the crowd and the noise both increased. ... boats were like to be five times longer a loading than they needed ... I was forced to goe from boat to boat ... for otherways some of the seamen would throw the souldiers overboard if they did not belong to them or the souldiers would have pressed into boats to have sunk them.[36]

Phips' expedition suffers severely from any comparison to European efforts of the same sort such as the English attacks on Gibraltar in 1704 or Barcelona in 1705. His effort was a poorly-executed scale model of this type, and certainly did not resemble forest warfare. In contrast, the Canadian scouting parties that encountered Walley's men fought like Indians, "... while the New England men taunted them as cowards who would never fight except under cover."[37] Phips' plan and tools were those of European wars. It was not scruples about honour, however, that had caused the *Bastonnais* to choose the siege rather then the savagery of war in the woods; it was a sound appreciation of the strengths, and weaknesses, of their colony. Failure hurt even more in these circumstances.

New England paid for her defeat. While *Te Deums* were sung with fervour in Canadian churches, God seemed to be whipping Phips' party all the way home with storms and frost. The Massachusetts government lost £40,000 in the venture, and the pious Puritans, like the Canadians, saw the fate of the expedition as the work of the Lord. Brooding on this judgment, and the search for the sin that had prompted it, were to contribute to the hysteria of the Salem witchcraft trials of 1692. Yet Phips' expedition had warned Canadians that raids would bring massive retaliation, and its failure had warned New Englanders that it was too costly to attempt to take Quebec without English support. This lesson the Americans learned well.

New York. Though hardly comparable to Massachusetts in strength, New York, alone, might have been a formidable opponent to Canada. Population favoured New York two to one. Geography, both human and physical, was kind to New York. The Lake Champlain route invited use of the superior manpower in a thrust at the heart of Canada, yet reduced defence costs to the protection of a narrow, fifteen-mile frontier at the confluence of the Hudson and Mohawk rivers, an area with easy communication and transportation links with all of the colony's resources. Politically, New York's short history as an English colony had been quite calm. Moreover, if undisputed gubernatorial power had any military advantages, New York also had these as there was no popular assembly. New York's economy was much more robust than Canada's; able to undersell the Canadians in the fur trade,[38] New York also conducted a sizeable export trade in flour, bread and pork. Even in times difficult for international or intercolonial trade, the New Yorkers would not go hungry. Involvement in the fur trade meant not only that there was a close relationship with the powerful Iroquois confederacy, but also that the ways of the woods were known to at least a few New Yorkers.

Despite these advantages, New York's defences failed disastrously at Schenectady in 1690, and the intercolonial land offensive of the same year dissolved in frustration. The call to arms in 1689 could not be heard in New York over the din of squabbling among New Yorkers. Indeed, all the advantages mentioned above dissolve upon closer scrutiny of the colony's problems.

About one-half of the white population of New York was Dutch. While language did not determine the lines of political faction in 1689, it did dilute enthusiasm for offensive operations in the name of the King of England, even if he happened to be Dutch. In the twenty-five years after the English conquest of this Dutch colony in 1664, New York had changed hands twice, with a minimum of violence; Dutch traders at Albany and Schenectady, and Dutch farmers on the upper Hudson were prepared to defend their property, but their loyalty to England or the English colonies could not be expected to outweigh self-interest. Both of New York's frontier towns, Albany and Schenectady, were predominantly Dutch[39] and when an English governor came to Albany to meet with the Iroquois, he found that the interpreters could translate only through Dutch. "More than one governor suspected rightly or wrongly that he and the sachems heard only what Albany wanted them to hear."[40] The New York frontier with Canada was left, somewhat unwillingly, to the Dutch.

New York, like Massachusetts, was a victim of its own politics in 1689. The exit of James II from England, and the imprisonment in Boston of Sir Edmund Andros, his Governor of the Dominion of New England, shook the foundation of royal authority in New York. Lieutenant-Governor Nicholson wrote to England from New York shortly before he lost power:

> It is most certain that the Governor of Canada will not slip this opportunity to Inflame those jalousies (sic) and by all fair & plausible meanes endeavour to unite our Indians to himself, wch would tend to the utter Ruin of all the English settlements on this Continent.[41]

Jacob Leisler, a well-to-do New York merchant, was one of the captains of militia who snatched power from Lieutenant-Governor Nicholson at the end of May, 1689. The question of the legitimacy of Leisler's government preoccupied New Yorkers for two decades after his fall, and has bedevilled historians of New York for more than two centuries. Small wonder that Leisler did not have full support from his fellow New Yorkers nor full co-operation from fellow colonies.

Albany, the crux of New York's defence against Canada, was the centre of the most vigorous and persistent opposition to the *de facto* government of the colony. Leisler and his colleagues had risen to power thanks to a political opportunity, but found their popular support based largely on economic promises. There was vocal opposition to the monopolies that controlled the colony's two major export industries, fur and flour. New York City merchants had a monopoly on bolting flour for export; Albany had a monopoly on the fur trade. Leisler's threat to abolish the monopolies was as welcome to the struggling new frontier post at Schenectady as it was unwelcome in Albany. Albany's defence of its fur monopoly rested largely on its responsible and informed handling of relations with the Iroquois. If all and sundry were allowed to trade with the Iroquois there would be fraud followed by revenge, and the result would be the ruin of the most important part of the colony's defences. So Albany did not yield in November 1689, when Leisler's chief lieutenant tried to convince the town to accept the new government. Even the horror of the Schenectady raid did not bring immediate submission, though it was crucial to the subsequent acceptance of support from New York City.

Albany's views could ruin the defence of New York, and New York's policy could ruin Albany. The economy of the colony might be versatile enough to survive war, but the fur-trading frontier town would find war disastrous. Albany much preferred to see the Iroquois hunting furs, rather than hunting Canadians, for two reasons. First, the Iroquois provided much of Albany's stock of furs by hunting—their role as middlemen in the trade has been greatly exaggerated.[42] When the Iroquois were not hunting in their own exhausted hunting territory, or poaching on the hunting grounds of their neighbours, they had nothing to trade at Albany. Second, illegal trade between Canadians and Albany merchants was a thriving business that war would make more precarious and less profitable. Some estimates suggest that more than one-half of Canada's beaver was shipped to Albany during Queen Anne's War.[43] By that time New York had been converted to Albany's viewpoint, a tacit neutrality that brought calm and profits while allowing the colony to spend less than one-eighth the defence costs of Massachusetts.[44] But, during the first war with Canada, Albany and New York were not able to withdraw, and Albany's fur shipments were reduced to less than a third of the earlier shipments; the town's population dwindled to two-thirds of that of 1689.[45] Like Canada, the fur town of Albany could not afford war. Unlike Canada, Albany would be able to avoid it after the Iroquois became neutral, in 1701. But, in 1689 Albany's troubles had just begun.

Defence was a key issue in the government of Jacob Leisler, his confidence and control within New York depended upon defence, and recognition from outside the colony hinged on successful defence. With powerful political enemies hurrying to the English court, Leisler was doubly sure that Schenectady had to be avenged. He called for an intercolonial conference to obtain aid and recognition—but Massachusetts, Connecticut, and Plymouth were the only colonies to send delegates.

New York's answer to the Schenectady raid was no muster of the colony's strength; it was a display of its weakness. New York's population should have afforded about 4,000 militiamen, close to the figure given by the colony's governor in 1687. He had added that the Iroquois would provide three or four thousand men.[46] Yet, at the intercolonial conference Leisler promised only 400 militiamen, while suggesting that nearly 2,000 Iroquois would join the cause. Both of these figures were pathetically optimistic; Leisler provided only 150 men, and only seventy Iroquois appeared after news reached the long houses of smallpox in the American party.

Connecticut was the only colony to send men to join the expedition. The full quota of 135 men promised by Connecticut was forthcoming, together with about fifty Indians from that colony, on the condition that their pro-Albany leader, Fitz-John Winthrop, lead the expedition. Winthrop had had a gentleman's role in the English army and led militia in his native Connecticut in 1672 and in King Philip's War without seeing much action.[47] He planned to lead an invasion force of nearly 3,000 men, forming one prong of the attack on Canada, while Phips' fleet formed the other. Instead, Winthrop led a party of about 400 men as far as Lake Champlain, taking more verbal shots at Leisler's government for inadequate supplies, manpower, and canoes, than he would take at the Canadians. At Wood Creek he discovered that there were only enough canoes for half of his party, and it was too late in the season to strip the birches to build more. What would have happened had 3,000 men come to Wood Creek? No more than did happen. The existing canoes were manned by about 150 volunteers, four-fifths of them Indians, and an expedition was launched under twenty-two-year-old Captain John Schuyler of Albany. They were able to beach their canoes at the northern end of Lake Champlain and to by-pass Fort Chambly, though not without being noticed. On August 23, 1690, the party attacked the hamlet of La Prairie, killing six men and taking nineteen prisoners, and leaving all houses, barns, and crops ablaze. Frontenac had been in the area with a force of 1,200 men two days earlier but had failed to discover the raiders. Schuyler's exploit encouraged the Iroquois to attack several isolated Canadian settlements, but it failed in its major strategic role of forcing the Canadians to move troops from Quebec to the environs of Montreal while Phips and his men attacked Quebec. Yet Schuyler had achieved something: New York had been avenged for Schenectady.

New York attempted a raid the following year. Organization was smooth by comparison; Leisler had been deposed and replaced by a royally-appointed governor, and other colonies were not involved in the plan. Mohawk and Mohican warriors joined Albany militiamen to form a force of about 400 men under Peter Schuyler, Mayor of Albany. As a raid on settlements, the expedition was a complete failure, since the crucial element of surprise was missing. The result was a bloody series of ambushes and close engagements. The New Yorkers inflicted heavier casualties than they received, but they retreated with the awareness that such endeavours were not worthwhile. New Yorkers would not return to the offensive for eighteen years, when an imperial and intercolonial expedition promised an overwhelming advantage in manpower and the objective was conquest.

* * *

By the end of 1691 the three North American contenders had found direct attack unprofitable. New York had found it nearly futile to fight garrisons when it had intended to terrorize hamlets. Massachusetts had found a siege of Quebec very arduous, expensive and disappointing. Canada, too, while the most successful in the initial exchanges, realized that attacks launched against New York and Massachusetts could provoke frightening counterattacks, rather than fear and confusion. The last five years of King William's War brought little direct action between the Americans and the Canadians. While the contenders were no less hostile towards each other, and defensive measures were necessary, the colonial war had de-escalated. New York and Massachusetts enjoyed relative calm; Canada directed its efforts against the Iroquois, and the English at Newfoundland and Hudson Bay.

The factors that produced a near stalemate early in King William's War did not remain constant for three generations. The political and administrative confusion in Massachusetts and New York was short-lived. Expansion and development changed all the contenders. Yet memory of the exchange of 1689-1691 fostered the illusion that the usable forces of English and French colonists were such that European assistance was necessary to achieve a decision.

It is not only as a chastening test of strength that the first phase of King William's War deserves attention. The strenuous efforts of these first three years indicate the type of war that each of the contenders found possible and necessary. In the next sixty-four years many things were to change, but the patterns of colonial conflict continued to show similarities with these initial encounters.

Chapter 2

Patterns of Colonial Conflict, 1692-1754

Even if the unity of the entire struggle for empire in America is emphasized, there are two significant ways in which the whole contest can be viewed. First, almost all the fighting in North America before 1755 was done by colonists. While the level of war seldom reached the intensity of the period 1689-1691, the motives, methods and objectives remained fundamentally the same until 1755. During this period the colonists engaged in a struggle limited to serving their purposes and capacities. Hence, fighting was sporadic and usually preoccupied with defence rather than offence. The nature of the contest would be revolutionized, after 1754, by the arrival of European troops, methods and priorities.

By stressing this particular change, another one is necessarily given less attention. There was a generation of relative peace (1714-1744) wedged between the two generations of war. Such a prolonged peace can serve as a natural division in any consideration of the whole struggle. Many warriors of the first generation had died before fighting was renewed. Populations doubled in the period of calm, and expansion and development altered the distribution of usable resources. Did this erode the memories and the hatreds, making the struggle from 1744 to 1760 essentially separate from that which ended in 1713? In this chapter the uneasy peace will be considered but the first way of viewing the total struggle, the way which focuses on the change in the pattern of conflict, will predominate.

KING WILLIAM'S WAR

After the exertions of the first three years of war, described in Chapter I, King William's War shifted to peripheral areas, and there Canada took the initiative. In the west, Canadian forces struck the Mohawk villages in 1693 and terrorized the Onandagas and Oneidas in 1696. Abenaquis, led by a few Canadians, struck the Maine frontier at York and Wells early in 1692, and they destroyed Oyster Bay, New Hampshire, in the summer of 1694. Pierre Le Moyne d'Iberville, a French-trained Canadian naval commander of outstanding skill and courage, struck the last significant blow of the war in the east, the conquest of Fort William Henry at Pemaquid, Maine. He also raided Newfoundland settlements and took Fort Nelson on Hudson Bay after a display of naval skill in a battle that pitted a single French vessel against three English. Although Newfoundland and Hudson Bay were on the periphery of Canada's war with the Americans, these areas were vital factors in a trade war with England herself.

The Treaty of Ryswick, in September of 1697, brought the War of the League of Augsburg to a close. North American issues may have received as much attention as they deserved in the broader context of the war, but that was very little attention indeed. Perhaps the stalemate in the colonial phase of the war was given recognition in the agreement to accept the *status quo* in America. Acadia, which remained in New England's possession for only a year, was officially restored to France. England gained advantages from her attention to Newfoundland and Hudson Bay in the closing months of the war. The treaty recognized the English reconquest of Newfoundland in 1697, and accepted English control of Hudson Bay, thereby invalidating Canadian gains made there after the peace was signed at Ryswick. The five-year peace ushered in by the Treaty of Ryswick was, in reality, a truce that allowed the combatants to gather strength for the next round of fighting.

QUEEN ANNE'S WAR

The North American version of the War of the Spanish Succession (1702-1713), known as Queen Anne's War, seemed to be a slow-motion rerun of the previous war. The colonial war opened belatedly in the summer of 1703, with Abenaquis raids on Wells, York, Saco, Winter Harbour, and Casco. Early the following year, the Canadians conducted a savage raid on Deerfield, Massachusetts. As well as sending Colonel Benjamin Church out against the Abenaquis in 1705, Massachusetts once again resolved to see Port Royal and Quebec conquered, though not without help from England. When two years had passed without this aid appearing, Massachusetts launched two raids on Port Royal, both of which failed. Two more years passed. In 1709, with a promise of help from England, New York and New England prepared for a re-enactment of the 1690 two-pronged attack on Canada. The English ships failed to arrive, and the North American expedition was postponed. The following season (1710), however, five Royal Navy vessels supported a successful New England attack on Port Royal.

The 400 marines sent out from Britain in 1710 were harbingers of greater British involvement in colonial wars. In 1711 Britain sent the Walker expedition to attack Canada—but not because of Deerfield or in fulfilment of their repeatedly-broken promises to help. A convulsion in British politics in 1710 brought men of Tory sentiment to power in Queen Anne's councils. These men were not happy with the length or cost of the war in Europe. They were also anxious to sponsor a hero of their own who might achieve a military victory that could offset the popularity Lord Marlborough's victories had given to the Whigs. Henry St. John, the Secretary of State who made the Walker expedition his concern, explained another aspect of the adventure to the governor of New York:

> Her Majesty is perfectly sensible how strong an objection would lye to the conduct of her councills, if at the end of so expensive and bloody a warr, the greatest burthen of which has layn upon Britain, she should be of all the confederates the only one who would reap no particular advantage, but be a sharer at large in the common benefit of reducing the power of France. We have exhausted ourselves with little or no concurrence from any of our allys to support the warr in Spain, as if we were singly concerned in the event of it. We have laid forth our utmost strength in the Netherlands, as if the obtaining that barrier was not an remote, but an immediate security. Gifts, loans and subsidys have been scattered from hence through the whole extent of the allyance, as if we were defending

provinces of our own, or as if we were ourselves a province to each, . . .

. . . .

The true application of what I have said is this, that it is now high time to do something in particular for Britain, by which the enemy will receive as great and as essential a prejudice, as he has done by any of those operations the sole benefit whereof resulted to some of our confederates.[1]

With purposes like these, fourteen ships of the line (all bigger than Phips' flagship) and thirty-one transports (there were only thirty-two vessels in Phips' whole fleet) were sent from Britain with 5,300 troops, including seven of Marlborough's veteran regiments. The armada left Boston with a striking force of nearly 6,500 men, while 2,300 men were working their way up the Lake Champlain route. Canada was being invaded by three times as many men as had threatened her in 1690, an attack by a force of almost half of the total population of Canada. The armada took little more than three weeks to get to the mouth of the St. Lawrence, but there nine vessels were wrecked in fog and gales, and nearly 900 men were lost. Though the fleet was still of overwhelming force, and though it was closer to Quebec than Phips had been by the last week of August, a council of war judged it impracticable for the Walker expedition to proceed to Quebec. Again the Lord was thanked in Canada, but this time New Englanders were not blaming themselves; they accused the British of frustrating a great design. As Walker's squadron went over the horizon, the war came to an end for the North Americans.

It is customary to decide who won a war by looking at the peace treaty, and the North American clauses of the Peace of Utrecht were catastrophic for New France. France ceded all claims to Newfoundland, except for fishing rights on the north shore. British control of Nova Scotia was accepted and, even if the boundaries were in dispute immediately, the major Acadian settlements were clearly under the British. Hudson Bay was recognized as British territory as well, though the limits of that claim were not settled either. France also agreed to a clause which implied British sovereignty over the Iroquois.

The terms of this settlement were not a just assessment of

the North American struggle. The peace was made in Europe, and made largely by Britain's Secretary of State Henry St. John, whose views on the war are quoted above. In light of these views, it should not be surprising that Britain deserted her allies to make a separate peace with the French, nor that the French had to pay for this less punitive peace with colonial and commercial concessions for the British. Marlborough had been right; the dash of a pen had yielded a great deal more than the Walker expedition had achieved. France itself was deprived only of those positions which were a constant challenge to the peace of Europe. It was New France which paid Louis XIV's debts at the bargaining table in Utrecht.

Britain won more for herself than for her colonies of Massachusetts and New York in the peace settlement. The cession of Hudson Bay was for Britain's trade. Britain would try desperately to monopolize the newly-won Newfoundland fisheries at the expense of New England.[2] When Phips had taken Port Royal in 1690, Britain had been willing to incorporate Acadia into Massachusetts, but after New England again took Port Royal in 1710, it was made a separate royal colony, Nova Scotia. New York was the only British colony to gain more than it had earned. Clause XV of the Treaty of Utrecht began:

> The Subjects of France inhabiting Canada shall hereafter give no Hindrance or Molestation to the Five Nations or Cantons of Indians subject to the Dominion of Great Britain nor to the other natives of America who are Friends to the same.[3]

Not only was the status of the Iroquois defined, but the same clause went on to grant all Indians the right to trade with French or English as they chose. This provision favoured New York, which was supplied with better and cheaper trade goods than were usually available through Canadian traders.[4]

Canada could have lost the Peace of Utrecht without losing the war. If the peace treaty was not an accurate measure of results in North American fighting, what other criteria are there? Casualties are very difficult to estimate, but it would appear that the Canadians and their allies inflicted casualties at a ratio of at least three to one. But anything less than a ratio of ten to one meant that Canada was still losing the manpower struggle with the Americans. Britain herself lost as many men off Egg Island as her colonies lost in a generation.[5]

Perhaps the military objectives of the colonial contenders can be used as a criterion of their success. Massachusetts had wanted to destroy French control of Acadia and Canada by conquering Port Royal and Quebec. Acadia was conquered twice, but Quebec was not taken. But is it fair to charge the *Bastonnais* with failure, when they were the only colonists who demanded such complete success and were ready to fight for it? New York's objectives were not as clear as those of Massachusetts. Governors of New York had advocated, from the mid-1680's onward, the conquest of Canada, but there had never been any question of conducting such a campaign without a great deal of outside help.[6] While waiting for ambitious plans to mature in London, New York was on the defensive. Raids like those of the Schuylers in 1690 and 1691 were retaliatory, to seek revenge and to maintain the reputation of New Yorkers with their Indian allies. Even while being auxiliaries to the unsuccessful invasions of Canada, New Yorkers had been quite successful in their secondary objective, defence of their frontier settlements and trade; there was no repeat of the Schenectady raid. Between 1691 and 1697 Canadian offensives on the western frontier avoided the colonists and focused on the Iroquois. From 1697 the whole New York frontier was becalmed for nearly fifty years.

Avoiding defeat is not necessarily victory, but survival was all Canada could hope for. There were daring schemes for the conquest of New York, but the main objective was to keep Massachusetts and New York on the defensive. Initially, the strategy was to terrorize the English colonies into paralysis. Far from achieving its goal, this prompted a massive counterattack. With the exception of the Deerfield massacre in 1704, this early policy was abandoned for a more effective one. Tacit neutrality on the New York frontier and Abenaqui raids on the Maine frontier kept the heart of New France safe and Massachusetts busy. The Canadian raid on Deerfield disturbed this balance and began a new outcry in the American colonies that led to the Walker expedition.

Canada survived because some of her enemies—the Iroquois

and the New Yorkers—came to prize survival, trade, and economy enough to becalm the Canada-New York frontier. Canada survived also because those opponents who actively sought to destroy her in 1711, as in 1690, were both incompetent and unfortunate. Canada avoided losing and, given the odds, that was winning.

UNEASY PEACE

The Peace of Utrecht was truly a peace, not a recess in a war, as the Peace of Ryswick had been. Western Europe did not return to general war for twenty-seven years—evidence of the stability possible because the agreement did not bring complete defeat or destruction to any of the main antagonists. Yet the peace was not self-perpetuating; it needed to be defended, and it survived only as long as its survival was desired by Britain and France. Not only did these powers refrain from war, they actively co-operated to keep peace. Though this Anglo-French *entente* seems particularly curious in the context of imperial rivalry, both sides found value in co-operation. For the British the arrangement meant some security against French support of the Jacobites, whose appeal showed such life in 1715. On the French scene, the duc d'Orléans, who became sole regent for the young Louis XV (in violation of the will of Louis XIV and in face of opposition in France and Spain) needed peace with Britain, too. The diplomatic accord established by Lord Stanhope and abbé Dubois was inherited by Robert Walpole and Cardinal Fleury, though there was little pacific in the objective of either power: "To utilize peace in order to procure for ourselves all the advantages of a large trade is to wage war on our enemies."[7] The peace reflected a balance of power that would eventually be disrupted by unequal economic growth, particularly evident in colonial trade, and by Spain's diplomatic migration from an aggressively independent foreign policy to an active alliance with France. The Bourbon Family Compact of 1733, formed between the ruling branches of the family in France and Spain, was closely linked with the outbreak of war for the throne of Poland; but the New World entered into the calculations as well. The British founding of Georgia in 1733 was as patent a violation of the *status quo* as was the Family Compact. It was already evident that the New World had become a more substantial ingredient in calculating any balance of power.

Was there an *entente* between Americans and Canadians to parallel the understanding between the British and the French? Almost everyone who had fought in North America before 1714 would not be involved when the fighting resumed. The colonials who were to fight were raised in an era of comparative peace. However, if competition for trade and for land can be called a quiet form of war, there was little peace in America. The unprecedented length of formal peace fostered sustained growth of almost all the settlements in North America; the continent which had been large enough to allow reluctant co-existence in 1713 was, by 1744, too small to permit it to continue. For North Americans the peace became an increasingly precarious truce. Unending reports of new Indian alliances, new fortifications, new settlements, and new trade routes could have conjured up the image of gladiators manoeuvring for position, yet hesitant to do more than feint, lest a misplaced blow should cost balance, position, perhaps everything. Tension was greatest on the southern American frontier where trade war, Indian war, and renewed French initiative in Louisiana came quickly after Utrecht. British and French spheres of expansion were even less defined there than elsewhere, and the situation, like that which later developed on the Ohio River, was therefore more volatile. Acadia, by contrast, was an old centre of conflict, with British conquest apparently confirmed by the peace of Utrecht. Yet, Acadian honesty about their loyalties to France and Catholicism, Canadian and French machinations to regain the colony, American suspicion and ambition, and British vacillation between conciliating and planning the expulsion of the Acadians, all combined to keep the eastern end of the Anglo-French frontier tense. Clearly, the European *entente* was not transported to the colonies, and the English and French imperial authorities themselves usually argued as though this fact was understood.[8]

The Yamassee War in the south (1715), and Dummer's War in the north (1722-1725) were primarily struggles between

American colonists and their Indian neighbours, but they interrupted the semblance of peace, and indicated the pressure of expanding American trade and settlement. The French founding of New Orleans (1718), the building of Louisbourg (started in 1720), the rebuilding of Fort Niagara (started in 1720) and the construction of Fort St. Frédéric (1731) was matched by the British construction of Fort Altamaha (1721), Fort Oswego (1727) and the establishment of Georgia (1733). Yet move and countermove were all just short of aggressive retaliation to destroy a new fort or colony. This restraint, which preserved the appearance of peace, was sometimes a result of the European *entente*. For example, a Canadian plan to attack the new American fort at Oswego in 1728 was abandoned when it was learned that the French court did not want to risk war.[9] Francis Parkman saw the essence of the New World situation when he wrote:

> The peace left the embers of war still smouldering, sure, when the time should come, to burst into flame. The next thirty years were years of chronic, smothered war, disguised, but never quite at rest.[10]

But when the war fires began to spread again in the New World, after 1739, they had been fanned from Europe, as before. Britain and Spain both went to war in America in 1739 to alter the terms of trade there. Britain was anxious to plunder Spanish America and, with French support, Spain challenged the aggressive intruder. British colonies became involved, of course. Georgia, by its very existence, was a contributing cause of the war, and the Anglo-Spanish frontier had serious raids. The major operation of the Anglo-Spanish War, and the only one to draw on substantial colonial support, was the Cartagena expedition (1741) under Admiral Vernon. Three thousand Americans, called such by the British for the first time,[11] joined what they thought would be a giant buccaneering venture. Instead of yellow gold, they found yellow fever, and more than half of the Americans died. Thus, another grand design of British imperial co-operation and conquest ended in disillusionment. After 1744, the war melted into the Anglo-French part of the War of the Austrian Succession.

KING GEORGE'S WAR

The North American version of the War of the Austrian Succession was more like a replay of earlier wars than a preliminary to the final struggle. As with the two earlier wars, the European monarchs gave the signal to commence hostilities. Once again the Europeans gave little support in the colonial theatre, and the colonists fought a good deal less than the full duration of the European war. In the hope of regaining Acadia, or at least obtaining supplies from the reluctant subjects of George II, the French governor of Louisbourg launched a successful expedition against Canso, Nova Scotia, in May of 1744. A former centre of New England fishermen, Canso had little

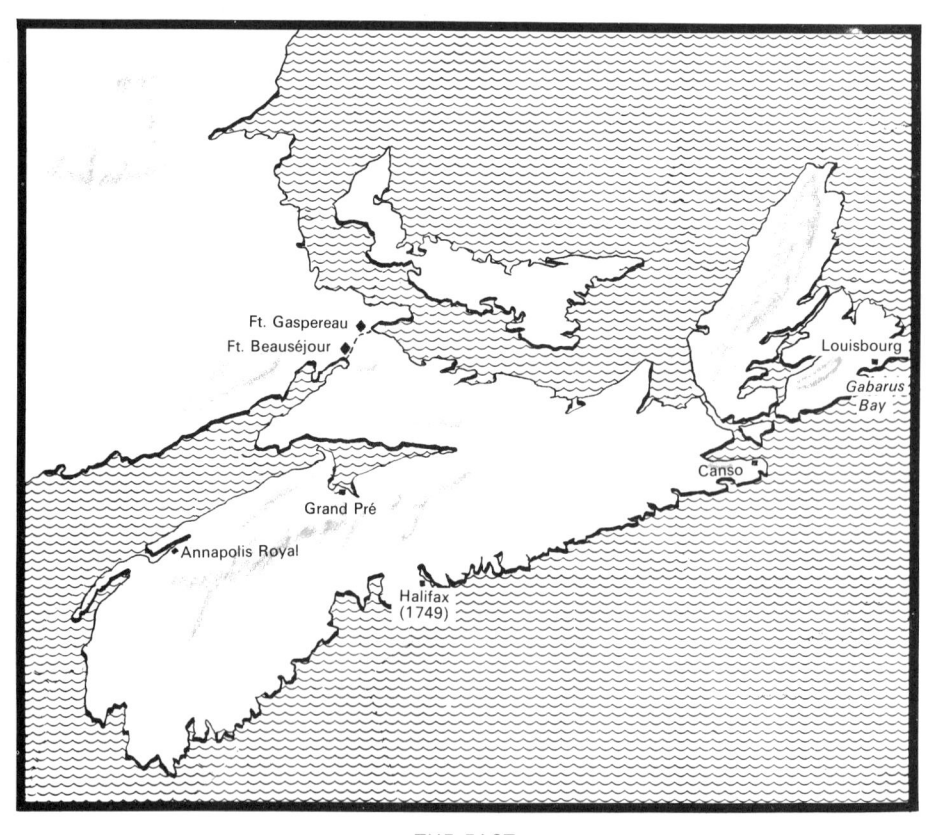

THE EAST

46 ❖ *Guerillas and Grenadiers*

inherent importance except as a minor British outpost which, if strengthened, could have severed communications between Louisbourg and Acadia. After this initial success came failure in a more ambitious attempt to take Annapolis Royal in July. A perceptive resident of Louisbourg, reflecting that the Franco-Canadian raid on Canso in 1744 had prompted the successful New England attack on Louisbourg (1745), said:

> It was the interest of the people of New England to live at peace with us and they would undoubtedly have done so if we had not been so ill-advised as to disturb the security which they felt in regard to us. They expected that both sides would hold aloof from the cruel war which had set Europe on fire, and that we, as well as they, should remain on the defensive only.[12]

New Englanders landing at Louisbourg, 1745. This English view somewhat exaggerates the formality of a campaign that was quite conventional.

Patterns of Colonial Conflict, 1692-1754 ❖ 47

Sir William Pepperell, New England commander at Louisbourg, 1745. This engraving was made two years later, when Pepperell was 51.

48 ❖ *Guerillas and Grenadiers*

The raid on Canso, like Frontenac's campaign of 1690, was a success which provoked an invasion. New England public opinion was outraged, New Englanders who were captured and taken to the fort at Louisbourg were impressed with the weakness, rather than the strength, of this famous French bastion, and Governor Shirley saw an opportunity to improve his political situation in Massachusetts by attacking Louisbourg.[13] In view of the prevailing opinion that an attack from landward would be very difficult, it is not surprising that Louisbourg had lavished most of its resources upon naval defence. Even so, it was a pleasant surprise for the 4,000-man New England force to discover that they were safe from the big cannon of the Grand Battery outside the walls. Once taken from landward, these guns were turned against the citadel itself and provided the firepower which worked most effectively against it. The siege was conducted by New England recruits led by a merchant prince, William Pepperell. Lack of experience or discipline were everywhere apparent; nearly half of the American casualties came from mishandling cannon.[14] Indeed, the siege was a caricature of European warfare conducted with levity, recklessness, and indiscipline. Good fortune was particularly necessary for the success of this sort of venture, and fortune was good to the New Englanders at Louisbourg.

Although the New Englanders considered the victory largely their own, they had been supported by £11,000 from the middle colonies — including £4,000 for supplies granted by Quaker Pennsylvania — and a British fleet under Commodore Peter Warren, which relieved Governor Shirley's apprehension that the colonial fleet would be too lame to support the landing force. Before the siege had ended, the British squadron which blockaded Louisbourg included twelve men-of-war and nearly 600 guns. French munitions for Louisbourg were captured and used against the city, and communication and supply lines to New England were secured. In the last analysis, the British squadrons blockading France made sure that Warren's squadron could command the entrance to Louisbourg.[15] The capture of Louisbourg was the British Empire's first major offensive against Canada to be successful.

Relations between the British and the Americans were relatively good at Louisbourg, largely because Warren did not impose his authority over Pepperell. A Louisbourg resident commented: "So striking was the mutual independence of the land army and the fleet that they were always represented to us as of different nations."[16] As with the 1710 assault on Port Royal, the fleet protected a land force which took a citadel. Ships' guns did not bombard Louisbourg—as those of Phips, Walker, and Saunders did Quebec—thereby minimizing Anglo-American co-operation to good effect.

The conquest of Louisbourg was the most significant action in the American war theatre; reactions to the event explain much of the rest of the war. New England and Britain were exuberant, although Secretary of State Newcastle was embarrassed by the conquest which made the French court less willing to negotiate peace. Just as the Walker expedition followed the capture of Port Royal, so 1746 was supposed to see a two-pronged invasion of Canada, with the rendezvous for the seaborne assault at Louisbourg itself. When the British fleet and eight battalions failed to arrive, the New Englanders could console themselves with the thought that the colonial troops raised in anticipation of the invasion were, for the first time, in British pay.[17] However, the encouragement of Anglo-American co-operation that resulted from the Louisbourg campaign was dispelled by the failure to attack Quebec in 1746.

While Britain schemed to build on the Louisbourg success, France was bent on reversing it. In the spring of 1746 an armada of seventy-six sail, including ten ships of the line, assembled at the French port of Rochefort. This fleet, under the Duc d'Anville, was able to slip through the British blockade before the end of June. The escape was more good fortune than might have been expected and, indeed, proved to be the only good news connected with this ill-fated squadron. The three-months' passage featured ferocious storms, deadly calms, and epidemics that cost 3,000 lives, including that of the commander. Like ghost ships, d'Anville's armada limped home from Nova Scotian waters without accomplishing anything; the death toll for the expedition had been higher than that of the whole war in North America.

Attack and counter-attack planned by the Europeans also caused feverish defensive preparations in English America. Troops raised and sent to the New York frontier for the invasion of Canada were hastily withdrawn when rumours reached New England of d'Anville's expected descent on Louisbourg, Annapolis Royal, and Boston.

Canada increased pressure on Acadia and the northern American frontier after Louisbourg fell. The missionary-warrior abbé Le Loutre used his influence with the Abenaquis and Micmac Indians to force more active Acadian opposition to British rule. A daring winter march by 500 Canadians, Acadians and Abenaquis led to the successful capture of the Acadian town of Grand Pré. Raids on frontier settlements in Maine, New Hampshire, and Massachusetts followed after the successful burning of Saratoga, New York's advance settlement north of Albany. Canadian reinforcements sent to Fort St. Frédéric when an invasion was expected went on to take Fort Massachusetts after the Anglo-American campaign of 1746 was abandoned. These raids, and renewed Abenaquis attacks on the Maine outposts along the Kennebec River, were blood-curdling echoes of the terror of half a century before.

At Aix-la-Chapelle, in 1748, the war in Europe was brought to a close with a peace comparable to Ryswick rather than Utrecht. North American issues were ignored, though colonial pawns were exchanged; Louisbourg, for all its importance and all the effort involved in its capture, was returned to France in exchange for Madras, India. The Europeans tried to keep the new peace in North America and cool colonial suspicions. For example, in 1753 Governor William Shirley was warned of French designs:

> But as it's His Majesty's determination not to be the aggressor, I have the King's commands, most strictly to enjoin you, not to make use of the armed force under your direction, excepting within the undoubted limits of his Majesty's dominion.[18]

In spite of European intentions, this was only a glorified cease-fire in North America, and war would resume there even before the European monarchs gave the signal.

Aix-la-Chapelle meant less to North America than had the formation of a land company, the Ohio Company of Virginia, a few months earlier. One event called for the cessation of hostilities, the other ensured that the fighting would resume.

THE WEST, 1754

CONFRONTATION ON THE OHIO

The Ohio Company of Virginia, which was granted a charter by the British government in 1749, was the first of a series of American ventures to develop Ohio lands, as well as trade with the Indians. Rivalries between groups of speculators and between colonies, as well as popular objections to land monopolies, severely hampered the Ohio Company. The main obstacle, however, was French determination to exclude all Americans from the Ohio Valley.

Canada had not shown much interest in the upper Ohio Valley before 1749, when it was put under the jurisdiction of the Canadian governor. Though explorers, missionaries and traders had long since travelled the Mississippi River, their route to the Mississippi had been through Lake Michigan and down the Illinois River. In the seventeenth century the upper Ohio had been Iroquois-controlled country—reason enough for the preference for the more westerly route. When penetration did become possible, the upper Ohio was no longer yielding quantities of prime furs. The Ohio's real value was to farmers, but these would come from British America, and New France could not allow the Virginians into that area without inviting a struggle that would become very unequal. The Appalachians had been a dike holding back the flood of Americans, but the Virginians were widening a crack with their road west of Wills Creek, a crack that could only be sealed by Canadian control of the forks of the Ohio in the name of the King of France.

The first attempt to establish the French claim to the upper Ohio was a somewhat quixotic expedition in 1749, led by Pierre-Joseph Céloron de Blainville. With a force of well over 200 men, Céloron travelled down the Alleghany River to the forks of the Ohio, down the Ohio as far as the Great Miami River, and northward up that river and across country to the French Fort Miamis, on the Maumee River, before returning home. During this circular tour of the territory being challenged, Céloron planted a number of lead plates bearing France's claim to the area. He also held conferences with the Senecas, Delawares, Mingos and Shawnees, as well as the Miamis. Céloron's demonstration of French strength was not completely successful;

Patterns of Colonial Conflict, 1692-1754 ❖ 53

his party encountered traders from New York, Pennsylvania and Virginia, occasionally in such numbers and with so many Indian friends as to make their ejection from the area impossible.

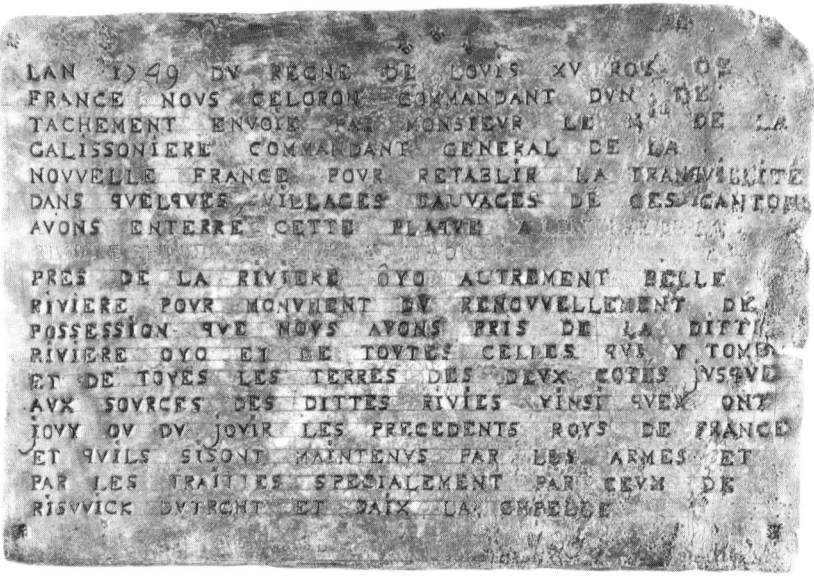

A Céloron plate, one of several which were planted by the Céloron expedition in 1749 to claim the upper Ohio Valley for the King of France.

Plaques did nothing to reinforce claims to the Ohio, and it was increasingly apparent that possession was the only meaningful claim. The initiative was taken in 1752, when Governor Duquesne had a fort built at Sandusky Bay, and a Miami settlement at Pickawillany noted for its friendship to American traders was destroyed by a Canadian and Indian raiding party. In 1753 the Governor had two posts, Presqu'Ile and Fort Le Boeuf, established between Lake Erie and the Alleghany River. The establishment in 1754 of Fort Venango on the Alleghany and Fort Duquesne at the forks of the Ohio completed the Canadian preparations for confrontation with Virginia.

Virginia's challenge to Canada, clear enough in the land dealings after 1749 and the arms build-up in 1751-1752,[19] was made explicit, in a rather feeble way, by the Washington mission of

1753. With a guide, an interpreter, a hunter, and an escort of seven men, three of whom were Indians, George Washington made a six-weeks' journey to the French commander at Fort Le Boeuf to deliver a letter from the Virginia Governor. The letter set out the British claim to the Ohio Valley and concluded: "It becomes my peaceable duty to require your peaceable departure." The commander commented in reply: "As to the summons you send me to retire, I do not think myself obliged to obey it."[20]

In November, 1753, Virginia's Governor was given British authority to use force, if necessary, to expel the French from the King's dominions. Whatever the western boundaries of the King's dominions, they certainly seemed to include the area at the forks of the Ohio granted to the Ohio Company by the King's charter. Washington was sent out to the forks of the Ohio the following spring with 159 men and promises of reinforcements from North Carolina, New York and several Indian tribes. The Indian warriors joined Washington's men in an ambush of a Canadian party, under Coulon de Jumonville, some forty miles from Fort Duquesne, but many of them joined the French and Canadian force when Washington's makeshift Fort Necessity was besieged in July.

Washington's position at Fort Necessity was an example of the confusion of guerilla and conventional warfare that would be a feature of the war which began with the ambush of Jumonville. The Virginia militia was armed with muskets and bayonets, not frontiersmen's rifles. Yet, their first military victory was an ambush that led French officers to charge Washington with the "assassination" of Jumonville. The building of Fort Necessity, and the defence of it, suggest the Virginians were reacting as European soldiers. On July 3, 1754, while the Virginians were digging entrenchments and fire pits in the mud around the weak palisade, a force of 500 French, Canadians, and Indians assembled under cover in a nearby woods. Judging the fort too weak, Washington formed his men into a firing line, in the open, in front of the fort and may even have begun an advanced toward the foe. War whoops from the woods may well have convinced some of the Virginians that this was not a contest between "civilized" enemies, for they soon scrambled for

Patterns of Colonial Conflict, 1692-1754 ❖ 55

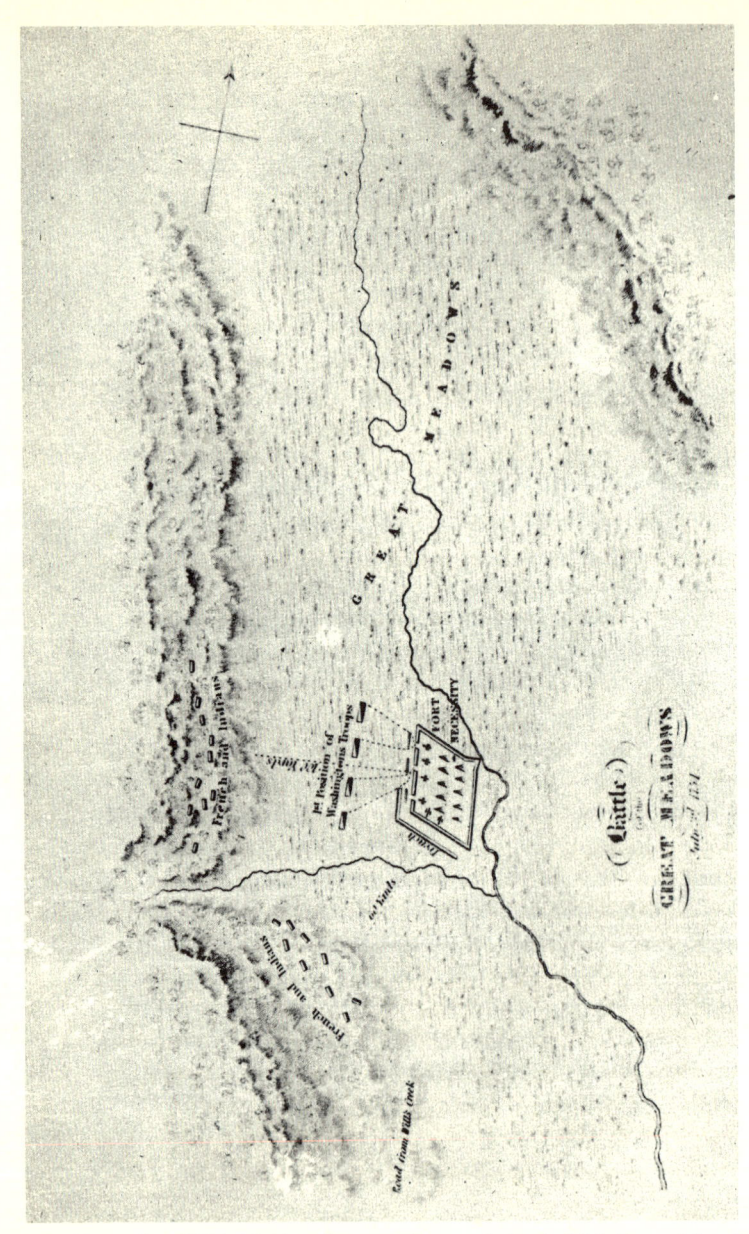

Fort Necessity, 1754. Notice the trenches and the initial line of battle drawn up in front of the fort.

56 ❖ *Guerillas and Grenadiers*

the meagre protection of their palisade. Fortunately for Washington and his men, this medley of types of war ended, not in a massacre, but in a surrender that allowed all of the Virginians to return home, save two hostages who were treated with the civility given European prisoners of war.

Virginians had attempted more than they could achieve; their unsuccessful attempt to lay claim to the forks of the Ohio touched off Indian raids in Pennsylvania, Maryland, and Virginia. They had alienated South Carolina officials by attempting to recruit warriors from tribes in that colony for the Virginian exploits without any reference to its government. They had frightened Pennsylvania traders with Virginian entry into the Indian trade of the Ohio, and they had disturbed all Pennsylvanians with the possible repercussions of the aggressive policy —loss of their few friends left among the Indians. Virginians had struck a spark, with tacit British approval, in a great deal of very dry tinder.

* * *

The Virginian initiative in the west was only one way in which the climax of the struggle would be different from the three colonial wars that had preceded it. In 1689, 1702 and 1714 the war between French and English colonists in North America began upon notification from Europe that it was time to go to war. The colonists had grievances and ambitions enough to promote the war, but the colonial phase of each war tended to start late, proceed intermittently, and end early.

The colonial contests before 1748 had more in common than the fact that, in all three cases, the starting guns were in Europe. New France struck the first major blow in each war: Frontenac's raids in 1690; the Abenaquis raids of 1703, and the Deerfield massacre the following winter; and the attack on Canso in 1744. This fact may have been coincidental. It may also have resulted from more centralized control, the Canadian ability to mobilize more quickly for a raid than the Americans could prepare for an invasion, the need for Canada to impress Indian allies by a bold attack, realization that frontiersmen and warriors were a great deal more effective attacking than defending, or an attempt to carry the war to the enemy so as to minimize the ravages and disruption in New France itself.

Each blow from New France at the beginning of hostilities prompted a major counter-offensive in the form of a siege of the major French fort in what would become modern Nova Scotia: Port Royal in 1690, 1707 (unsuccessful), and 1710; Louisbourg in 1745. Though British assistance became increasingly important in the attacks of 1710 and 1745, these sieges were inspired by New England and fought by New Englanders. These offensives were retaliations for the frontier raids and the attacks of privateers on New England shipping and fishing. These offensives were also a part of New England's political and economic expansion.

Each siege in Nova Scotia was linked to the siege of Quebec City. The smaller siege was a military and psychological prerequisite for the larger. To test the strength of New England and New France, to secure supply lines and retreat from Quebec, and to encourage New England investors and the British government that victory was possible, the New Englanders had to take Port Royal or Louisbourg. Each successful siege in Nova Scotia was then followed by an unsuccessful attempt on Quebec City: Phips in 1690, Walker in 1711, and the scheme that failed to mature in 1746.

Whether by coincidence or necessity, the first three colonial wars had a pattern of conflict that maintained an equilibrium between the contenders. Canada seldom had plans and never had hopes or means to destroy British America. On the other hand, the inconclusive nature of strenuous attempts to conquer Canada reinforced the parochial and defensive attitudes of the American colonies. However unequal the contenders, these wars preserved the balance of power in North America. Neither side displayed sufficient power to conquer, although both had the power to retaliate.

Signs of change in the pattern of North American war can be seen in considering the contest for the Ohio country after 1749. By 1754 colonists of England and France clashed in the wilderness over the claims of their kings, and themselves, to the upper Ohio. The shots were not heard around the world, though the French government advertised the "assassination" of

Jumonville in Europe. Nevertheless, this clash, and its aftermath, would draw France and Britain into a gigantic struggle in North America and for North America. For the first time the New World called the Old to arms.

The most significant portent was not necessarily the obvious one, that New World issues erupted into war while Europe was at peace. The fight on the Ohio marked the entry of Virginia into the struggle with Canada. Virginia was interested in a specific tract of land for settlement. Virginia was the most valuable trading partner in Britain's American seaboard, and Virgina's initiative was in defence of King George II's charter and in compliance with instructions from the British government to the Governor of Virginia. The most significant sign of the transformation in colonial warfare was this British consent to Virginia's fight. When the Virginians were in difficulty this consent helped to bring substantial British aid to America in the form of the British army.

PART TWO

GUERILLAS AND GRENADIERS
1755-1760

Chapter 3

Battle Array, 1755

The nine-year-old Mohawk boy who watched the warriors prepare for battle in 1689 hardly resembled the scarfaced, seventy-five-year-old Chief Hendrick who fell in battle near Fort St. Frédéric in the summer of 1755. The struggle that engulfed him had changed as much as he had, and some of the most significant changes in warfare were occurring during the summer he died. Not only had the strength and involvement of the contenders of 1689 been altered by sixty-five years of expansion and development, but new contenders and new contests were altering the nature of the fight. The Ohio frontier had already exploded; moreover, 1755 marked the beginning of a direct, substantial, and continuous British commitment of men, money and ships to the North American war. The two British regiments under General Edward Braddock may be viewed as ushers of this change. The new scale of British commitment prompted an even bigger French response. In reviewing the conditions of the various contenders in 1755, by way of a background to the climax of the struggle for Canada, it is useful to keep in mind this fundamental change—the Europeans had come to fight in North America.

CANADA

The peace of Utrecht had brought wondrous expansion for New France, and the War of the Austrian Succession had resulted in relatively little real damage once Louisbourg had been restored to France. The population of Canada had tripled after 1713 to more than 55,000 in 1755, this despite the lack of immigration of any consequence and several epidemics that cost as many as 2,000 lives each. New farmlands had been opened up along the Ottawa, Richelieu and particularly the Chaudière rivers.[1] Though a Swedish traveller might marvel, in 1749, at the extent of wild no-man's-land between Fort St. Frédéric and the English Fort Nicholson on the Upper Hudson,[2] this buffer of less than fifty miles provided no security in comparison with the 200-mile zone that had existed in 1689. (See above p. 17.) Now field armies could and would grapple at Lake George (1755), Fort William Henry (1757), and Fort Carillon (1758). Canada had done more than New York to destroy the old buffer, yet the forts and even the Canadian offensives would be essentially defensive—to protect Montreal and Quebec.[3] While the pattern of Canadian expansion suggests the continued importance of water transport, road-building allowed expansion back from the waterfront and provided communications links of vital military significance. Water routes were still definitely superior to roads, but in some circumstances roads were quicker. For example, a return trip by water from Montreal to Quebec might occasionally take as much as a month, whereas the trip could take as little as nine days by coach over the road that had been completed in 1735.[4] This road was to be the colony's lifeline when a British fleet invested the St. Lawrence in July of 1759.

Despite their value, the network of roads around Quebec and Montreal solved an infinitesimal problem of communication compared to the colossal task of marshalling all of New France as it was supposed to be marshalled under the governor-general at Quebec. It may seem quixotic for France to have attempted to gird a continent, from refurbished Louisbourg with over 3,000 men[5] to Louisiana, where 1,350 troops gave courage to the scattered settlements of less than 5,000 souls.[6] Yet American colonists had shown fear of a French encirclement from the beginning of the century,[7] and the barrier was much more real in 1755 when a chain of forts from Lake Erie to the Ohio had been completed and successfully defended. William Shirley glanced at the impressive French achievement in February of 1755:

> . . . His Majesty's Colonies upon this Continent are surrounded with the encroachments of the French, they have long since marked out for themselves a large Empire upon the back of it, extending from Cape Breton, to the Gulf of

Mexico, and Comprehending the Country between the Apalachian Mountains and Pacific Ocean, with the numerous powerful Tribes of Indians inhabiting it, and they are now finishing the extreme parts by a communication between Louisbourg and Quebec, across the Isthmus of Nova Scotia and Bay of Fonda, at one End, and a Junction of Canada with the Mississippi by a Line of Forts, upon the great Lakes and Rivers, at the other.[8]

While there was much concern in the American colonies about "encirclement," a perceptive ex-governor of New France was not so satisfied with the state of French control of the interior. Roland Michel Barrin, marquis de la Galissonière, touched at one vital weakness in a report of 1750. The colonies of Louisiana and New France:

> ... cannot send nor receive anything except by sea, and by the mouths of two rivers more than nine hundred leagues distant, whatever course be taken. The interior of the country is liable to be exposed to great scarcity of goods from France and to be glutted with its own products should a maritime power such as England, undertake to blockade the only two outlets of that vast Continent.[9]

The Canadian link with the grain producing Illinois country was real, but Louisiana remained too far away to allow an exchange of letters with Quebec, overland, in much less than a year. In addition, "encirclement" had given the opponent the interior lines of defence and the opportunity to marshal troops for a variety of possible objectives. For instance, the Anglo-American forces gathered at Albany in 1755 and in 1758 could have been destined for an attack upon Montreal, Fort Frontenac or Fort Niagara. While complete surprise was unlikely because of the length of the journey to any of these targets, the deployment of Canadian defences was made much more difficult by the changes in the geography of war since 1689. It was fortunate for Canada that the pattern of American rivers east of the Appalachians made full use of "interior lines" difficult.

The precariousness of Canada's elongated frontier is attested by the string of forts from Louisbourg to Fort Duquesne which had no other purpose than defence. Every fort in this tremendous and tenuous chain was built to correct a weakness, and many of them would be weaknesses themselves, particularly when British cannon were turned on what were only trading posts grown into wooden forts. Niagara, Fort Chambly, Fort Carillon, Fort St. Frédéric, Louisbourg, and Quebec were the only forts in the European sense.

Another problem was that the odds against Canada of half a century before had not been altered by the growth of French Canada—the American colonies had grown apace. Moreover, although the 8,000 men of the colony could be mustered into a militia, fewer of them were familiar with woodland warfare than had been the case in 1689.*

One source of help in this situation was France, and, for the first time in nearly a century, 2,000 French regulars under baron de Dieskau arrived at Quebec in 1755—France's answer to the Braddock expedition. (See below, pp. 84-87.) While it is usually assumed that British troops and American militia did not mix well, the existence of the same situation north of the American colonies has not always been appreciated. Dieskau would be captured before the end of the year, and the Canadian-born Governor of Canada, Pierre de Rigaud, marquis de Vaudreuil-Cavagnal, would urge that no new general be sent out, as the demands of war in America were unlike those of Europe; in particular, the small colony could not afford to treat lives as cheaply as did French commanders.[10] The arrival of Louis-Joseph, marquis de Montcalm-Gozon, as the replacement for Dieskau, was not the beginning of a close working relationship between him and the Canadian Governor. While the French soldiers were considered a mixed blessing from the start, because of precarious grain supplies, the situation reached the point of being a French occupation of Canada when Montcalm was put above the Governor in the last months before the conquest.[11]

Indians were the other major source of manpower for Can-

---

*About 13,000 people, nearly one in four Canadians lived in the three centres of Quebec, Montreal, and Trois Rivières in 1735, whereas only one in five Canadians had lived in these centres in 1689, when they were much smaller and less sophisticated.

ada. No reliable figures on Indian population in this period are possible, but a conservative estimate of the number of warriors in tribes north of the Ohio friendly to New France in 1750 is in the neighbourhood of 16,000.[12] The French Ministry of Marine showed some misunderstanding of past policy, and some appreciation of the state of affairs in 1752 in arguing:

> ... 'tis considered proper to direct M. Duquesne to lay down henceforward in Canada a different system from that always followed hitherto in regard to wars among the Indians. With a view to occupy and weaken them, the principle has been to excite and foment these sorts of wars. That was of advantage in the infancy of the settlement of Canada. But in the conditions to which these Nations are now reduced, and in their present dispositions generally, it is in every respect more useful that the French perform between them the part of protectors and pacificators. They will, thereby, entertain more consideration and attachment for us; the colony will be more tranquil in consequence, and we shall save considerable expense.[13]

While the Indians had hoped for a balance of power between British and French in North America,[14] they were no longer able to hold that balance themselves, as had been possible a half-century earlier. Indian negotiators had to "pick the winner" to defend themselves and the supply of trade goods that was by now vital to their survival. The realities of their situation gave no choice to some tribes, such as the Micmacs and the remnants of the Abenaquis. The Iroquois at least had the freedom to be neutral, though it is hard to see how they could have given more than promises to Canada. In the west, however, the situation was different. When the supply of French trade goods for the interior had been cut off during King George's War, Indian support for the French had waned. In 1747 an Indian conspiracy had threatened to oust the French from the Ohio Valley, but this situation had been redressed by the vigorous policies of Governors La Galissonière and La Jonquière after the Peace of Aix-la-Chapelle and by the Canadian victory over Washington in 1754. Thomas Pownall, former governor of New York, praised the maternal French approach to the Indians as giving them command of the continent in 1755:

> They have thus thro'out the Country 60 or 70 Forts & almost as many Settlements, which influence the command of this Country, not One of which without the above true Spirit of Policy could they support with all the Expence & Force of Canada. Not all the Power of France could, 'tis the Indian Interest alone that does maintain these Forts.[15]

But New France would need to win consistently to maintain Indian alliances, especially since the British blockade of the St. Lawrence had already begun. Not only would most tribes follow the winner, but they could only make a significant contribution as long as Canada was on the offensive. Indians would continue to be helpful as scouts and guerilla fighters, but were prudently suspicious of the European war games that culminated in open field battles to defend forts which did not defend the soldiers.

Manpower was one vital ingredient of war always in short supply for New France; the other was the economic means to furnish an army. Despite the long peace, political stability,* and the kind of administrative initiative associated with the long intendancy of Gilles Hocquart, the Canadian economy was as precarious in 1755 as it had been in 1689. Although shipbuilding, iron mining and smelting, sealing, weaving, and lumbering were fostered, and some trade developed with the French West Indies and Louisbourg, Canada exported more than she imported in only three of the nineteen years between 1730 and 1749. After 1749 the heavy deficits only grew larger.[16] Fur retained its primacy in the economy of New France with a system of trading posts and forts that reached far beyond the empire of the Ohio or Mississippi to the Saskatchewan and the Missouri. Inflated prices increased the yield of the trade, though the number of pelts stabilized after 1737.[17] Successes in out-

---

*The elder Marquis de Vaudreuil was governor for more than 20 years (1703-1725), as was his successor, the Marquis de Beauharnois (1726-1746). Gilles Hocquart was intendant for 17 years (1731-1748) and the Minister of Marine under whom he served, Comte de Maurepas, was in office even longer (1723-1749).

flanking the Hudson's Bay Company, by the establishment of new posts in the western interior, had been offset by the strengthening position of Pennsylvania traders in the Ohio country.[18] The battle for furs was still a part of the battle for New France.

More grain than gunpowder was needed to defend Canada and, after the British blockade began in 1756, most of the grain had to be Canadian. Yet there were eight crop failures in the last twenty years of New France, including three in a row, 1756-1758. Whether grain shortage was the result of soil exhaustion, subdivision of the strip farms along the rivers' edges, the maintenance of 3,000 French troops, the disruption of agriculture due to militia service as far away as the Ohio, the price fixing and forced sales instituted by the peculating Intendant Bigot, or just plain bad weather, grain was a continuous problem from 1755 to the fall of Quebec.[19]

Hopes that the Illinois country, which supplied grain for Louisiana, could do the same for Canada were never realized.[20] The grain situation imposed its demands on the strategy of New France in the Seven Years' War. For example, because of the shortage of supplies and the need to have the militia home in time to take in the harvest, military successes at Oswego (1756) and Fort William Henry (1757) remained isolated incidents and did not become starting points for deeper penetrations into British-held territory. The Canadians faced a cruel dilemma: they had to retain the initiative in order to protect the crops, but they had to withdraw early, in order to harvest the crops. While they could not push the offensive far enough to do more than prolong the war, neither could they afford to be thrown on the defensive, for the British regulars had no need to break off their offensive in August to go harvesting.[21]

If one were to attempt to single out one man as responsible for the fall of New France François Bigot, Intendant of New France, would be as likely a candidate as James Wolfe or William Pitt. Although the year 1755 saw the beginning of the disintegration of Bigot's first group of French business and administrative figures, called *la Société du Canada*,[22] it had already sapped the fiscal strength of the colony and would soon be supplanted by another Bigot syndicate known as *la Grande*

Société. Since 1748, when Bigot had become Intendant, he and his fellows had made fortunes at the expense of the Canadian people and the King of France. The sharp rise in prices (25 percent to 40 percent between 1751 and 1755) was certainly helped by the activities of Bigot and his associates.[23] Canadian merchants were ruined, and some left the colony before the fall of New France. Colonial resentment against Frenchmen was not confined to the military; Bigot's brand of buccaneering was resented, too.

As accountant for the deficit-ridden government of New France, Bigot had made claims of an unprecedented size on the French government during and after 1748. By the middle of 1753 these amounted to three and one-half million livre, prompting royal threats that all would be repudiated if the rate of expenses was not cut and, finally, the threat to give up Canada if the expenses continued.[24] The Court proposed a poll tax in 1754, but this scheme was dropped; the King continued to pay the deficits to the end of the regime.[25] By 1755, with the first hints that the French government was learning about the activities of *la Sociètè du Canada* and signs of serious war from the south, members of Bigot's group, including the Intendant, began to petition the home government for transfers and recalls "for the good of their health."[26] The King would get his revenge, for some fifty accused were eventually tried in Paris and, after a three-year trial, the royal treasury was reimbursed for twelve million livre.[27] The sentences did less to their fortunes than they had done to the fortunes of New France.

Was Canada as prepared for war in 1755 as she had been in 1689? While expansion had robbed her of some of the geographic advantages enjoyed in 1689, fortifications had been built in an attempt to lessen this change. If the sixfold increase in American population between 1689 and 1755 meant that Canada needed a force six times as large as that available in 1689, the Canadian militia, Indian allies and European troops (regulars and *troupes de la marine*) were nearly sufficient. Of course there are qualifications: there were comparatively fewer *coureurs de bois* in 1755 and with the fur trade extending deeper into the continent they were farther away from the likely areas of military activity; garrison duty in the widely-scattered forts used men who could not easily be mustered for a unified operation; Indian alliances were even more precarious than before; grain supplies were more difficult to acquire for these larger forces; and friction between French and Canadian forces, stemming from different concepts of war, represented a threat to co-operation and efficiency. The economy of New France was almost as weak as in 1689, though for different reasons. In 1755 Canada was also weaker *vis à vis* her traditional American enemies than she had been in 1689—in spite of the aid of French regulars. Yet, the real weakness of Canada in 1755 was that she had not only to fight traditional American enemies, but new opponents, both American and British, as well.

THE AMERICAN COLONIES

Prosperity and expansion for Canada's southern neighbours meant progress from strength to strength. German and Scots-Irish migrants arrived in increasing numbers after the 1720's to roll back the frontiers of Pennsylvania, Maryland, Virginia and the Carolinas, and to help swell the total American population to approximately one and a quarter million by 1755. Villages had become cities; Philadelphia, for example, now ranked among the largest cities in the British Empire. Even so, the rural population continued to grow at a faster rate than the urban.[28] The frontier was receding so rapidly that a traveller in 1749 claimed that one could go inland 120 miles in most areas before finding Indian settlements, and live half a year in the coastal towns without ever seeing an Indian.[29] By 1754 a regular stagecoach service operated between New York and Philadelphia. An efficient postal service was serving colonies from New England to Virginia by the following year.[30] The Appalachians could not stem the tide of American expansion, and it was very questionable whether Canada could or France would. It was no longer possible to shrug off the incredible disparity in population by pointing out American disunity and provincialism. Even if they were not united, almost every colony from Virginia north was now involved in opposition to New France, either in self-defence or because of designs on new lands.

Expansion altered the human geography, and with it the military geography. Despite the expansion of American colonial frontiers, relatively few Americans were now frontiersmen. One British writer lamented the colonial situation in 1757:

> Our people are nothing but a set of farmers and planters, used only to the axe or hoe.—Theirs are not only well trained and disciplined, but they are used to arms from their infancy among the Indians; and are reckoned equal, if not superior in that part of the world to veteran troops. . . . These [Canadians] are troops that fight without pay—maintain themselves in the woods without charges—march without baggage—and support themselves without stores and magazines—we are at immense charges for those purposes.[31]

Indian tribes on the Anglo-French frontier, including the most powerful allies of Canada and New York (the Abenaquis and the Iroquois respectively) lost land and relative strength. As the Indian buffers weakened, the European antagonists came to face each other more directly at the watersheds of the Chaudière and Kennebec, the Richelieu and Hudson, the Ohio and the Potomac systems.

The unity of New France bound together what otherwise could have been a series of separate struggles, and involved most of British America as a result. Though Canada's heartland still had its geographic ramparts, the Americans now had the interior lines of defense against a Canadian defense line running from Louisbourg to Fort Duquesne. The advantage was evident in the success of the Monckton expedition of 1755 in capturing control of the head of the Bay of Fundy, thereby isolating Louisbourg. While General Braddock would not succeed in attempting a similar thrust at Fort Duquesne, the key to the Ohio Valley, the British strategy in 1755 attempted to use the advantages of their interior position. American supply lines generally were capable of being protected easily, and new farmlands on the frontier were able to help supply armies with more speed than if supplies had had to be carted from the coastal centres. Thus, while Canada held the offensive on her extended frontier, geography was less a friend than it had been before, or would be again once Canada was thrown on the defensive.

The seriousness with which the American colonies took their situation, and the situation itself, were revealed at the Albany Conference in the summer of 1754. The conference, attended by the delegates from seven colonies, was initially called to co-ordinate colonial dealings with the Iroquois, who had grown sullen and hostile enough to cause fears of their defection to New France. The Iroquois grievances concerned Albany's trade with Canada which, they said, resulted in Albany providing the Canadians with guns and ammunition that were used against the Iroquois. They also complained that greed and chicanery had come to dominate the Americans' land purchases. At the conference thirty wagonloads of presents helped to improve relations, as did the subsequent appointment of William Johnson as sole custodian of Indian relations on the northern frontier. But, before the convention concluded, the delegates went much further than soliciting good will from the Iroquois; indeed, most of the legates went beyond their powers by approving a plan of military and political union for the colonies, which they thought should be imposed upon British America by a British act of parliament. They may have been visionaries, but the bad-tasting remedy they prescribed grew out of a realistic appreciation:

> ... that the colonies were seldom all in equal danger at the same time, or equally sensible of it; that some of them had particular interests to manage, with which a union might interfere; and that they were extremely jealous of each other; it was thought impracticable to obtain a joint agreement of all the colonies to a union. ... [Therefore] it was necessary the Union should be established by act of Parliament.[32]

The British administration, on the other hand, felt the initiative would have to come from the colonial governments.[33]

Though the Albany Conference did not succeed in uniting British America, it clearly demonstrated that these colonies were closer together and much stronger than they had been in 1689. Communications had improved. Expansion had forced more colonies into conflict with New France, even though it had also caused quarrelling among Americans. A united American effort was not achieved at Albany, but the co-ordinating of strategy under a British commander-in-chief did much to draw together British America's war effort.

With more colonies committed to war against Canada than in earlier wars, the resources available for war came closer to being the full resources of British America. Nine colonies with larger populations than that of New France, gave America a manpower advantage of nearly twenty-five to one. The foodstuffs of British America seemed limitless; the Governor of Pennsylvania, for example, claimed in 1755 that his colony alone could export enough food to provide for an army of 100,000 men.[34] The colonial iron industry, centred in Pennsylvania, was so well developed that it was able to compete effectively with British manufacture. Rich and burgeoning British America had increased the overwhelming superiority over New France that it had possessed in 1689. Yet it was Virginia, not Canada, that received assistance first from Europe in 1755.

EUROPEAN CONTENDERS

As if in retaliation for three calls to arms from Europe, the shots that rang out near Fort Duquesne in the summer of 1754 signalled the beginning of the fourth and last Anglo-French contest for a continent. Of course, Europe's Seven Years' War did not start in America. It was not because of the shots in the forest-shrouded wilderness that Britain's long-standing alliance with Austria ended in 1755, or that Britain concluded a new alliance with Frederick the Great of Prussia in January, 1756. It was this new alliance that drew Britain into the Seven Years' War proper when Frederick invaded Saxony at the end of August. None the less, Britain had already been formally at war with France for more than three months. In May, 1756, King George II gave the obvious reasons for the recent declaration of war with France when he addressed parliament:

> The injuries and hostilities which have been for some time committed by the French, against my dominions and subjects, are now followed by the actual invasion of the island

of Minorca, which stands guaranteed to me by all the great powers in Europe, and in particular by the French king.[35]

Minorca, which was not without its significance in naval defence of the New World, was the immediate grievance, and behind it stood the American contest. Britain and France were fighting for empire, in America, the West Indies, and in India. That they changed European partners before formally resuming the fight was important to the course and outcome, but not to the outbreak of the Anglo-French war in 1756.

Britain   As New World events edged them towards a war that would be global, British ministers were reluctant to see it coming. The Duke of Newcastle, the central figure in the ministry in 1754, wrote:

> Tho' I hope and think that the present disposition of the French Court is so pacific that if we take care of our rights and possessions in North America, by either building forts on our boundaries to render theirs useless, or else by demolishing such as may have been clearly and notoriously built upon our ground, that will not produce any disturbance but be matter of debate and negotiation, wherein they will be the complainants, as we unfortunately have hitherto been.[36]

The British government backed into its tremendous commitment in America. The ministry planned to support Virginia's Lieutenant-Governor Dinwiddie* after 1755 by bringing two companies of regulars from New York and one from South Carolina to man newly-built forts, for which the British made a substantial contribution of £13,500. This figure was raised to £20,000 when it was learned that Duquesne had captured the partially-finished Virginian fort that would bear his name. News of the defeat of Washington at Fort Necessity caused real confusion, but this was cleared away by the plan to send General Braddock to Virginia with two Irish regiments.[37] To keep

---

*Robert Dinwiddie (1693-1770) was an English administrator in the customs service in America from 1727. He was Lieutenant-Governor of Virginia from 1751 to 1758.

the American plans of his shaky ministry from parliamentary attention, Newcastle reorganized the ministry to secure a Commons majority. Newcastle also planned to avoid parliamentary grants by financing the Braddock expedition with a budget surplus of £100,000. Finally, the throne speech emphasized that peace was being preserved in Europe without saying much of America. One parliamentarian objected:

> Is not this nation a part of Europe? Can it be said, that our affairs have received no alteration, when it is so well known that the French have actually attacked us, and have murdered a great number of our people, as well as robbed many others, in America? I call it murder and robbery, Sir, because it was done without any declaration of war; and it is a mere sophism, unworthy even of a minister, to say, that no alteration has happened in Europe, because this happened in America.[38]

Before the parliamentarians could be stopped they had revived the debate on whether the war with France could best be served with or without a European ally. There was something in the question:

> What signifies it, Sir, to talk to us of the numerous armies of France? Can they come to Britain, can they be sent to America, whilst we have such a superiority of naval power? .... we have there [America], I believe, twenty men to their one, and unless we have very much degenerated from what we were in the days of our Edwards and Henrys one Englishman may always be reckoned at least equal to one Frenchman.[39]

This question had logic, but what ministry could abandon Hanover to French armies and keep the confidence of George II, its Elector? As for the sabre-rattling, it sowed seeds of support for an aggressive policy in America, seeds that would be nourished by the outcome of the 1755 campaign in America.

If the European struggle for North America is represented by the distorting simile of a trial of strength between an expert swordsman who could not swim and an expert swimmer who could not fence, the overall strategy of both is obvious. The swimmer (Britain) wants to swim first and fence later (in America) as surely as the swordsman (France) wants to fence first (in Europe) and swim later.

Britain's fleet was expected to serve the insulating function of blockade that was traditional policy, and the navy also was to perform the newer and more difficult task of landing and actively supporting British troops in the New World. In 1756 Britain had 130 ships-of-the-line, more than twice the fighting strength of the French navy.[40] This force, with its scores of supporting frigates and smaller craft, could afford to maintain a powerful blockade of the French Atlantic ports, thereby protecting the British merchant marine and British colonies, as well as preventing any French invasion of England. In addition, there could be powerful squadrons for duty in the New World.

Early in 1755 there was no war in Europe, and no need for the "Western Squadron" off the coast of France, but the use made of fleets in the New World indicated that Britain was willing to bring war to Europe. France sent some 3,000 regulars to Louisbourg and Canada that summer. A week before these troops left Brest, a British squadron of twelve men-of-war under Vice-Admiral Edward Boscawen* left for America where he was to add the ships then in American waters and take his enlarged squadron to cruise in the neighbourhood of Louisbourg and the entrance to the Gulf of St. Lawrence.

> And in Case you should meet with any French Ships of War, or other Ships, having Troops, or Warlike Stores on board, you shall use your best Endeavours to seize and secure the same; And in Case any opposition shall be made to your so doing, you will use the Means in your Power to take and destroy them....[41]

*Edward Boscawen (1711-1761), had served in the Royal Navy from 1732, taking part in the attacks on Porto Bello (1739-1740) and Cartagena (1741). In 1747 he was made commander-in-chief in the East Indies. He became a commissioner of the Admiralty in 1751 and vice-admiral in 1755. The climax of his career was still to come. He commanded the fleet in the siege of Louisbourg (1758) and in the important naval victory at Lagos Bay (1759).

This order may seem a curious one in peacetime, but both sides seemed to expect trouble. The convoy for the French troops was so strong that it suggests that France expected interference. The British ministry felt Boscawen's squadron was too weak, and seven more ships were sent out as reinforcements. As the *Alcide*, first of two French ships to be captured, was being overhauled by the *Dunkirk*, the French captain asked: "Be we at war or at peace?" and Captain Howe* of the *Dunkirk* replied: "At peace, at peace." Moments later his order sent a volley of cannon and musket fire into the French ship, causing eighty casualties, putting cannon out of action, shredding the rigging with chain shot, and in the process shedding the mask of peace that had shrouded the beginning of the war. Despite Boscawen's fleet, all but two of the French ships managed, with the help of fog, to get through his net; he captured only ten of the seventy-eight companies of French regulars bound for Louisbourg and Canada. His bad luck was repeated when the same squadron slipped past him again on the way back to France. It might have been some comfort for him to know that a British squadron, authorized to open naval hosilities in European waters, also missed both de la Motte's fleet and another one that brought Montcalm and 1,000 regulars to New France early in 1756.[42] The British naval net would tighten, but France had succeeded in delivering four times as many troops to America as Britain had sent in the last months of European peace.

France The French ministry was as reluctant as the British to accept the fact that war was coming. When, towards the end of

---

*Richard Howe (1726-1799) had, at the age of fourteen, sailed as far as Cape Horn with Anson and had been active in the war of the Austrian Succession. Yet, his career was only beginning with the capture of *Alcide* in 1755. He would distinguish himself as an officer at Cherbourg and St. Malo (1758) and in the blockade of Brest and the battle of Quiberon Bay (1759). After a peacetime career in naval administration, he became vice-admiral and commander-in-chief in North American waters during the American Revolution. After a brief retirement, he commanded at Gibraltar (1782), became First Lord of the Admiralty (1783-1788) and Earl Howe (1788). In the war with Revolutionary France he won the important sea battle of June 1, 1794, in the Channel.

1754, Governor Duquesne sent a list of the warlike activities of his neighbours, he ended:

> After the assassination of M. de Jumonville and the above consequent proofs, do you believe, my Lord, that I am authorized to anticipate a rupture [of the peace] on the part of the English?

The Minister of Marine's reply was "No."[43] It was almost as though the French ministry was accepting the old notion of "no peace beyond the line"—that hostilities outside Europe did not affect the peace of Europe—as was Newcastle. (See above, p. 75.) In 1775 this concept could only favour Britain. France had three times Britain's population* and ten times her army, but she had little more than half Britain's navy.† France could certainly not allow Britain to fight behind the shield of her fleet without fighting in Europe. The traditional way to lure Britain out of her element was for France to invade the Netherlands, from which an invasion of Britain could be threatened. But in 1756 France's neighbour in the Netherlands was Austria, a new-found ally. Nevertheless, a lame threat of a direct invasion of Britain from the French Channel ports, and the threat of the British King's territory of Hanover were enough to ensure the linking of the war at sea with the continental war to contain Prussia.

For the French, the New World war was at best a holding action (like that which had been common to Britain and France earlier). (See above, pp. 11-12.) to await the successful outcome of a European struggle. Throughout the struggle, despite the enormous increases in the Anglo-American forces, Canada did not have more than 6,600 French regular troops; 4,000 of these came out before June of 1756. There were two important and related reasons to support the logic of a limited commitment in the New World, finances and the tightening net of British sea power.

While the assumption of substantial military expenditures in

*Though statistics are not available, the figures would be in the neighbourhod of 6,000,000 for Britain and 20,000,000 for France.
†France had 67 ships-of-the-line, England 130. Graham, *Empire of the North Atlantic*, pp. 146, 153; Mahan, *The Influence of Sea Power Upon History, 1660-1783* (Boston, 1890), p. 29.

America was unusual for the British, France had long been investing government monies in Canada—perhaps too long. Impressive forts and impressive private fortunes had been built at the king's expense. As mentioned in discussing New France, the governor and intendant were told, in 1754, that if government expenses in Canada continued at their present level, not only would the bills not be paid, but the colony would be abandoned.[44]

Financial difficulties were not confined to the Canadian bureaucrats, for the French navy was still heavily burdened with debts contracted before 1748, for which funds had not been allowed. The navy began with a financial disadvantage and never recovered.[45] So did Canada, both in her own limitations and those imposed on the navy.

The French navy had been substantially enlarged, in spite of financial difficulties, between 1749 and 1754, but there was no miracle like that which had been performed earlier by Colbert. (See above, pp. 12-13.) France maintained the superiority in naval architecture that led many a British commander to make a French prize vessel his flagship. But the Franco-Spanish combined naval force was still inferior in numbers to the British fleet. Numerical inferiority and lack of funds both dictated a defensive naval policy. A British court martial ordered an admiral shot* for the kind of defensive action from which his opposite-number could deviate only at his peril.†

Sending troops and supplies to Canada entailed very serious risks for the French navy, even as early as 1755. In this context, Lieutenant-General de la Motte's successful landing of General Dieskau's troops represented both ministerial determination to send some help to Canada, and extensive good fortune in accomplishing its task. De la Motte's fleet, like Dieskau's force,

---

*Admiral John Byng (1704-1757) was shot by order of court martial for his defeat at Minorca in May of 1756.

†La Galissonière's instructions included: "The object that he must keep always foremost in his mind is the preservation of the forces which His Majesty has detailed for this expedition. It is with this end in view, that His Majesty wishes him to direct all operations necessary to attain the required objectives. The intention of His Majesty is that neither his squadron nor his troops should be risked against superior forces." Quoted in Graham, *Empire of the North Atlantic*, p. 148.

was the largest attempt to reinforce Canada in the whole war. The action taken by the minister in December, 1758, as the assault on Canada became a certainty, seemed more in keeping with the French naval strength and necessary priorities. It would take the whole French fleet to escort aid to Canada, the ministers argued, and this would risk "la marine entière de Sa Majesté, Sans certitude du succèz."[46]

At the end of 1755, however, France could still feel satisfied with the assistance rendered to Canada, for the limitations of her naval strength had not yet shown its result. The string of fortresses that defended Canada, the regular troops who played an important role on the Monongahela and Lake George that year, and the money that made it possible for every defender of Canada, be he French, Canadian, or Indian, to do his part—these were the contributions of the King of France to the defence of Canada. Failure of the British offensive of 1755, and the success of the Canadian offensive in 1756 and 1757, helped to postpone full realization of the severe limits imposed on French assistance to New France.

Chapter 4

Braddock's Offensive, 1755

In April of 1755 the Virginia frontier town of Alexandria was bustling and overcrowded. Major-General Edward Braddock, a tough veteran of that élite corps of Britain's army, the Coldstream Guards, had arrived with two regiments of British regulars. These were not the only visitors. On April 14 Braddock held a conference at Alexandria attended by Admiral Augustus Keppel, commander of Royal Navy vessels in North American waters, by the Governors of Virginia, Maryland, Pennsylvania, New York and Massachusetts, and by William Johnson, the leading Indian agent for the northern colonies. Braddock revealed the basic strategy as stipulated in his instructions from the British government. London had decided *what* was to be done, and the conference discussed *how* it would be done.

The object of Braddock's offensive was to take four French forts: Fort Duquesne, Fort Niagara, Fort St. Frédéric and Fort Beauséjour. As far as the British were concerned, as Braddock commented, this plan ". . . takes in all the considerable Encroachments the French have made upon His Majesty's Dominions in America, . . ."[1] In assessing the campaign, it must be remembered that England and France were at peace in 1755. At no time was Braddock considering an attempt to conquer Canada; his offensive was supposed to roll back the edges of France's empire in America.

Braddock's offensive bore the stamp of conventional warfare; the objective of each of four Anglo-American armies was to take a fortress. However, the kind of force to be used in each of these operations was different. The attack on Fort Duquesne was to involve British regulars and southern colonial militia. Fort Niagara was to be taken by American volunteers in two new British regiments, together with Iroquois and militiamen.

Colonial militia, rangers and Iroquois were assigned the task of seizing Fort St. Frédéric. Finally, a force of New England volunteers, together with a small number of British regulars were to serve under a British commander, Colonel Robert Monckton, in attacking Fort Beauséjour. Indian and ranger units in these armies constituted almost all the trained guerillas in the Anglo-American forces. Therefore, the mixing of guerillas and the more conventional regulars and militia was most significant in the Fort St. Frédéric campaign. Since these four

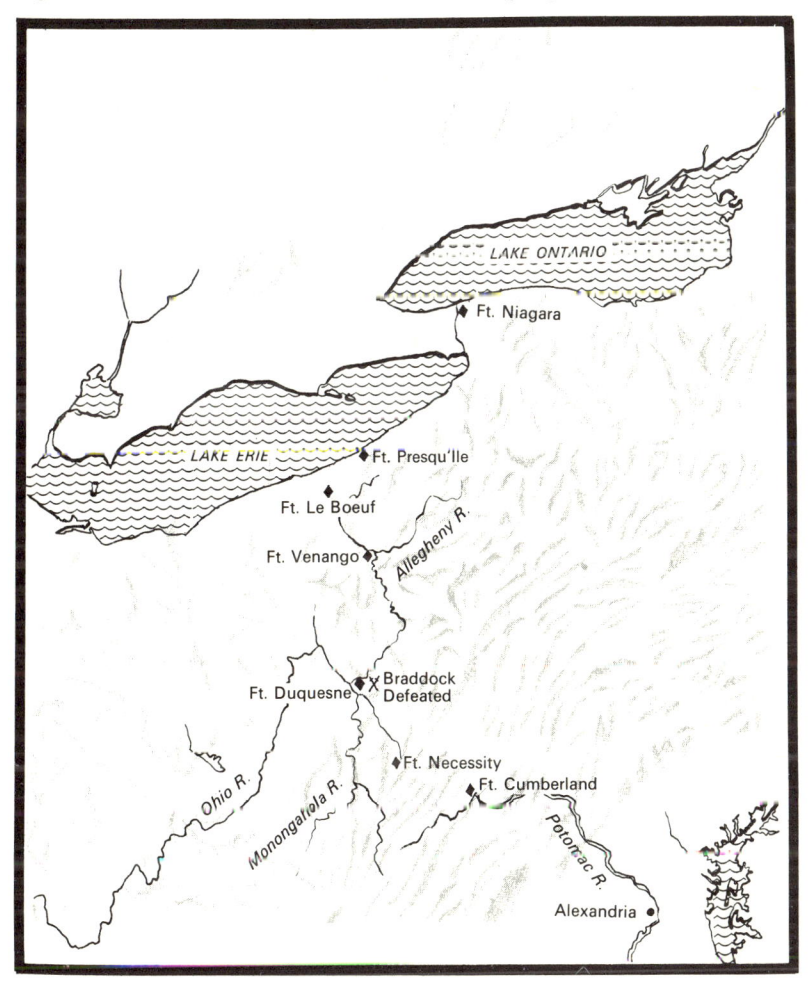

THE FORKS OF THE OHIO, 1755

campaigns were undertaken by different kinds of armies, some clues as to the type of force most effective for this kind of task can be gleaned from the experience. In addition, the four expeditions were not all financed in the same manner. Thus Braddock's offensive can provide the student of this war, as it should have provided the British government, with information useful for comparison and analysis.

FORT DUQUESNE

Fort Duquesne was the primary objective of a force led by General Braddock himself. Braddock had brought two Irish regiments, reinforced to a total of 1,000 men, to Virginia. Four hundred Virginians were recruited into these regiments, so that, when British-paid Independent companies from New York and South Carolina were added, something approaching 1,600 men drew salaries from the British treasury. Nearly 1,000 militiamen from Virginia, Maryland and North Carolina brought the striking force to about 2,500 men. Where were the Indian allies? Lieutenant-Governor Dinwiddie, who was better at convincing the British government to attack Fort Duquesne through Virginia than he was at giving them accurate information, promised a powerful auxiliary force of Catawba and Cherokee; but he so alienated the South Carolina government concerning negotiations with these Indian allies, that none at all appeared.[2] Dinwiddie also misled the British government and Braddock into believing that Washington's route of 1754 was the best approach to Fort Duquesne, when it patently was not. As a result, Braddock's force endured a long march over the mountains—cutting roads, dragging cannon and supplies. A French commentator at Fort Duquesne said the journey was forty-eight leagues (about 150 miles), but "... worth twice that distance ..." because of the terrain and definitely "... could not be accomplished in one campaign...."[3]

After a two-month effort an advance force of 1,450 men marched into disaster a few miles from their destination, Fort Duquesne. Seventy-two *troupes de la marine,* 146 Canadian militiamen and 637 Indians including Shawnee and Mingo warriors, until recently English allies,[4] had set out to ambush the forward party, but were too late. After a moment's surprise and confusion, with *troupes de la marine* and the British van trying to form firing lines on a road twelve feet wide and flanked with underbrush and trees, the Indians and Canadians melted into the surrounding cover on both sides of the road. From a hill commanding the road, from a ravine that crossed it, from brush everywhere, a rain of musket and rifle destroyed Braddock's army—a better ambush could hardly have been planned. Virginian frontiersmen who dove for cover met concealed opponents and died. Of 1,450 men, 977 were killed or wounded, including General Braddock who received a mortal wound after having five horses shot out from under him. The Indian, Canadian and French force suffered but twenty-three killed, including the commander, Beaujeu, and sixteen wounded.[5]

Braddock's expedition failed for a variety of reasons. Blame can be apportioned to Governor Dinwiddie for urging the wrong route and for bungling Indian relations. The commander of the van, Thomas Gage, failed to scout adequately—the textbook rules for European soldiers would have sufficed in this instance. Of course, the commander-in-chief was ultimately responsible for everything. He had brought his army to its destination with speed and determination, but when the firing started he was surprised and confused enough not to insist that the column be halted until the trouble was understood. Beyond that he was only guilty of reacting like a European commander, which surely is not surprising for a man who had spent forty-four years in a European army. It would have been much more surprising if he and his men had been able to master the essentials of guerilla warfare in those few chaotic moments they had left.

Battle of the Monongahela, 1755. Plate I (page 86) shows the situation as the battle began. Details are identified as follows: a. French, Canadian and Indian force; b. guides and light horse for Braddock's force; c. vanguard; d. advanced party; e. working party; g. wagons of tools and ammunition; n. main body; q. flank guards; r. ravine; s. hill (without flank guards). Plate II (page 87) shows the situation during the battle. Details are identified as follows: f. abandoned field pieces; p. rear guard, now sole defenders of the wagon train; "c, d, e, h, i, k, m, n, q, the whole body of the British [and Americans] joined, with little or no order, but endeavouring to make fronts towards the Enemy's fire." Both sketches are by Patrick Mackellar, engineer *en second* on Braddock's expedition.

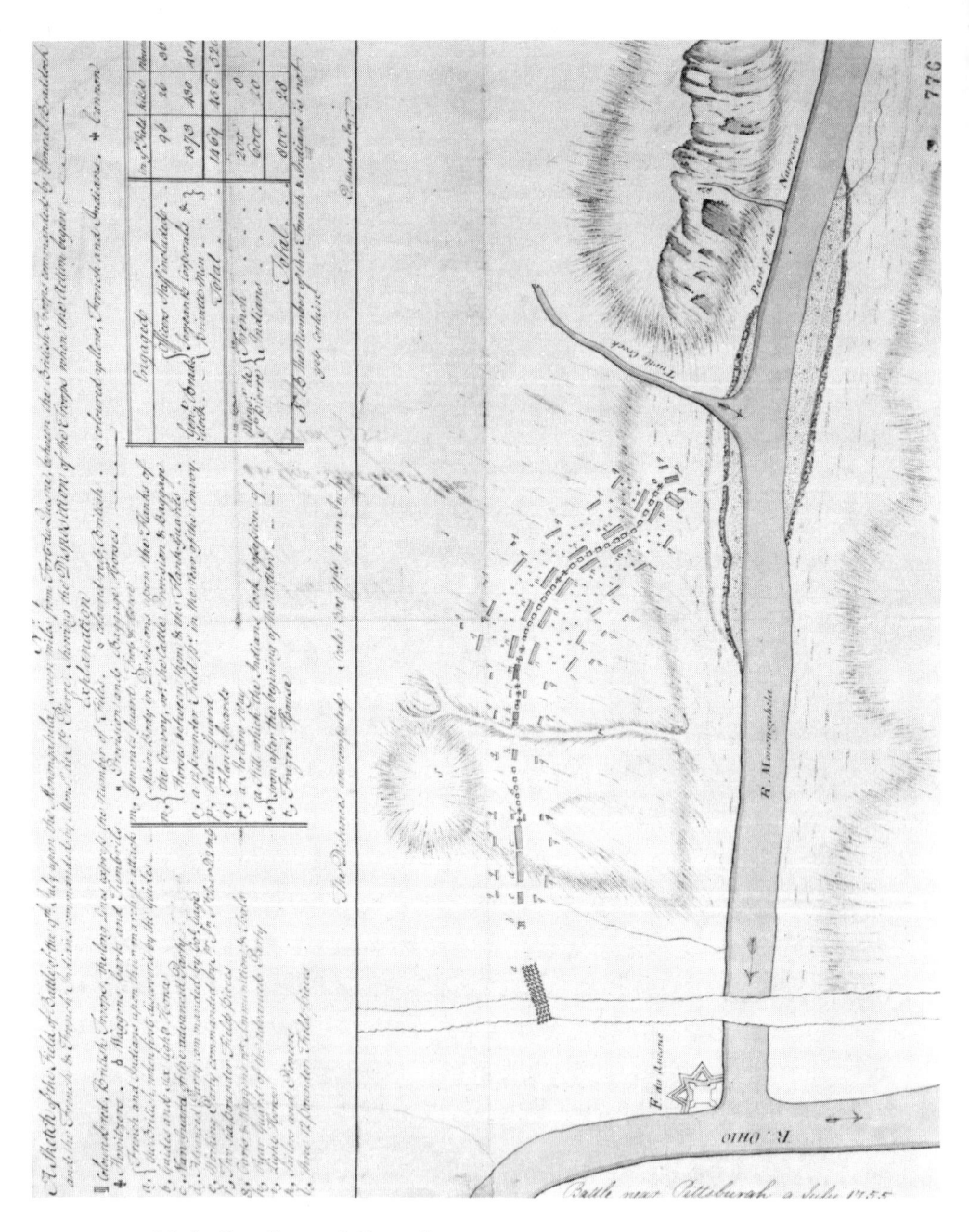

86 ❖ *Guerillas and Grenadiers*

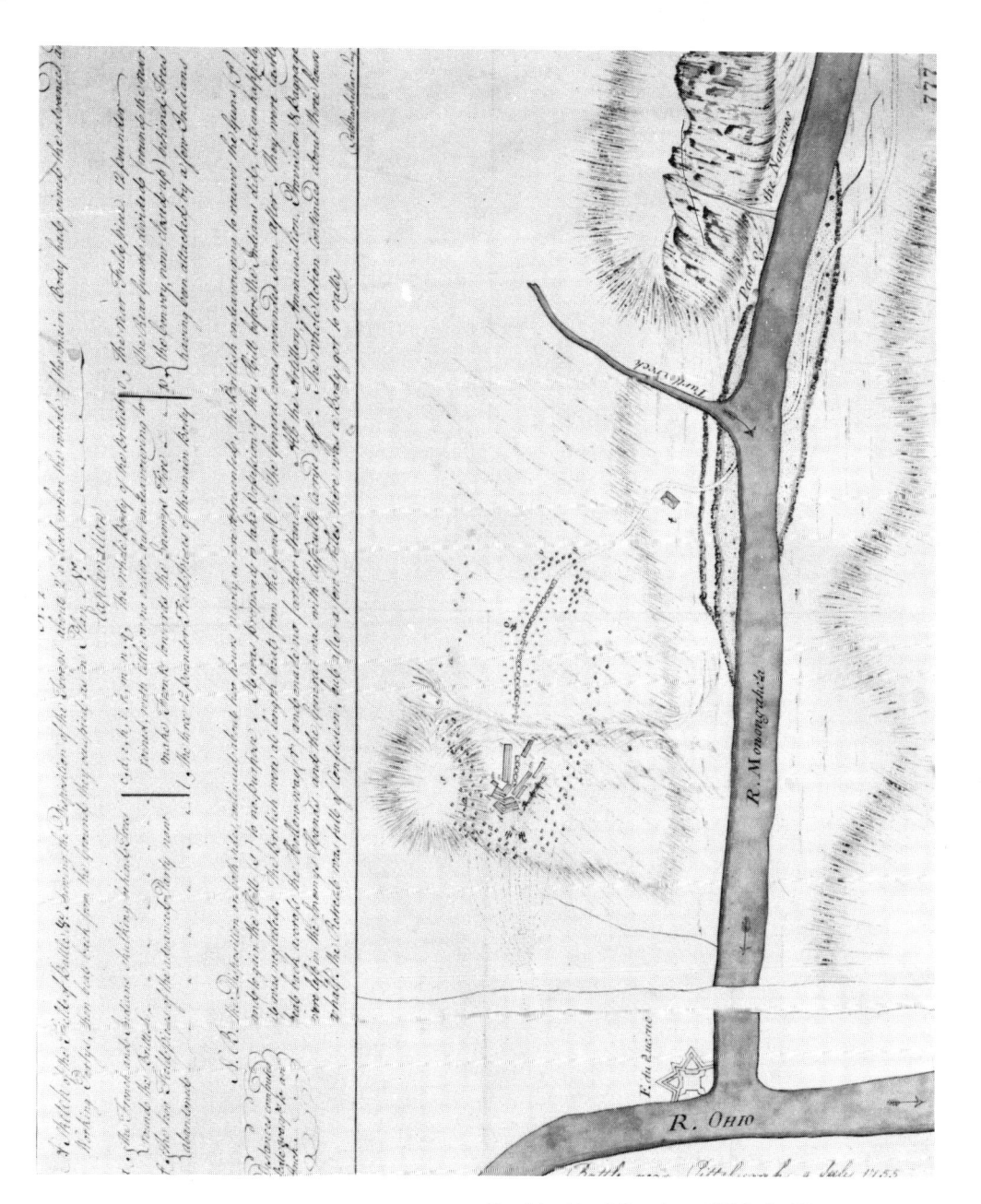

Braddock's Offensive, 1755 ❖ 87

Even after this disaster it would have been possible to push on to Fort Duquesne with a good chance of success, but Colonel Thomas Dunbar made sure that all had been in vain by sending the army off to winter quarters—in July. Though Braddock's wrangles with colonial assemblies, in an effort to gain funds for supplies and wagons, had little direct bearing on the military fiasco, they undoubtedly emphasized the delays and restrictions which came from dependence on colonial funds.[6]

FORT NIAGARA

Upon Braddock's death, William Shirley, Governor of Massachusetts, became commander-in-chief in America. His part in the 1755 operations, as agreed to at the meeting with Braddock in Virginia that April, was to involve attacks on Fort St. Frédéric (which he had strongly recommended himself) and Niagara (which New Yorkers, including William Johnson, had attempted to have adopted as Braddock's first objective). Shirley took personal leadership of the Niagara campaign, involving a 400-mile expedition that included a descent of the treacherous Oswego River, where experienced boatsmen

> . . . thought it less Risk of hanging for Desertion, and leaving the Battoes and lading than of drowning, by running down the several Rifts and Falls.[7]

After its arrival at Fort Oswego, the expedition was to travel to Niagara by boats to be built on Lake Ontario.

The forceful Shirley met serious opposition from the Lieutenant-Governor of New York, James Delancey, whose connections with local merchants made him resent Shirley's granting of the lucrative army contracts to merchants outside Delancey's circle. As chief executive in New York, Delancey did not appreciate the Governor of Massachusetts leading a military expedition within his jurisdiction. From quibbling over Shirley's use of New York cannon, the feud spread to complete non-co-operation. This, of course, only aggravated the serious supply problems inherent in Shirley's operation. A further difficulty was a growing rift between Shirley and William Johnson, who believed Shirley was trying to destroy him and his force. Johnson, therefore, refused Shirley's request for some

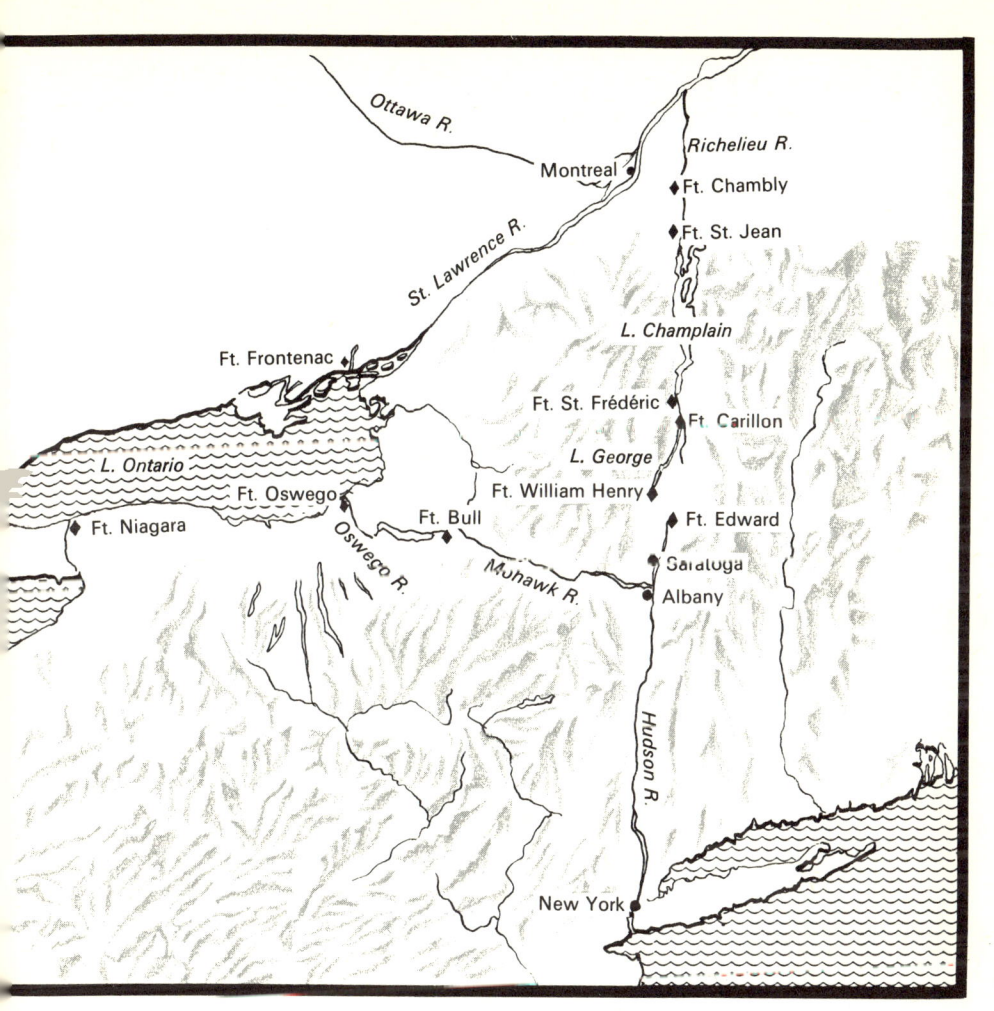

THE CENTRE, 1755

Indian support, complained of him repeatedly, and attempted to run an independent campaign.

Though 2,000 of Shirley's 2,500-man force were wearing the King's uniform, they were untrained colonial troops of the newly-raised regiments under Shirley and Sir William Pepperell, accompanied by a regiment of New Jersey militia and 100 Indians. The arduous journey west of Albany, and the sad news from the Monongahela accounted for some 800 desertions by the time the force reached Oswego. There the crumbling fort had to be repaired, lest it invite attack from the 1,200 men across the lake at Fort Frontenac. Shirley would have taken serious risks if he had proceeded to Fort Niagara in spite of the strong force across the lake. A Franco-Canadian attack on Fort Oswego in Shirley's absence could have succeeded in taking the fort and in leaving Shirley's army without supplies or a line of retreat. The lateness of the season, bad weather, and fear of French strength as troops drifted down the waterway from the west towards winter quarters, all helped to ensure Shirley's failure to do more than reinforce Fort Oswego. The British government, paying all the bills save the salaries of the New Jersey militia, gave credence to Shirley's unjust critics that winter.

FORT ST. FRÉDÉRIC

The offensive against Fort St. Frédéric (Crown Point) was a colonial effort to an even greater extent than Shirley's operation. Not only were the troops colonial, they were militiamen paid and supplied by colonial assemblies. This arrangement certainly added nothing to the speed with which the expedition got under way. It was early August before the commander, William Johnson, and the last of three contingents of his 3,500-man force left Albany. Johnson was a Mohawk Valley pioneer and fur trader. His contingent, most of whom provided their own weapons, included some 300 Iroquois led by tough old Chief Hendrick, as well as Robert Rogers, famous later as the Rogers of the Rangers, among the scouts.[8] Here, if anywhere in the major actions of the war, one might expect a demonstration of woodland warfare, at least as far as circumstances would allow.

The task at hand was not, however, one for frontiersmen. The expedition included a siege train of sixteen cannon to bombard Fort St. Frédéric, some weighing nearly three tons. On reaching the end of water transportation, 1,500 men were detailed to rebuild an overgrown road from the site of Fort Edward, the building of which was now begun, to the south end of Lake George, some fifteen miles away. In little more than two weeks Johnson was encamped on Lake George, leaving a small garrison at the unfinished Fort Edward. When Johnson's scouts brought news of a large French force in the vicinity of Fort Edward—vital to his supply and retreat—1,000 men were sent out to engage this force, or perhaps to strengthen Fort Edward. The French force in question was General Dieskau's, 200 regulars, 600 Canadian militiamen and 700 Indians, who showed a strong preference for an attack on Johnson's camp rather than on a fort. When Baron Dieskau learned of the 1,000-man expedition:

> I immediately made my arrangements, ordered the Indians to throw themselves into the woods, to allow the enemy to pass, so as to attack them in the rear, whilst the Canadians took them on the flank, and I should wait for them in front with the regular troops.[9]

Although the trap was sprung prematurely by over-anxious warriors, the leader of the American expedition and Chief Hendrick were among those killed in the first exchanges, and the rest were chased back to Johnson's camp, now fortified with rude defences. Dieskau, copying the successful tactics of the Monongahela fight, had shown that European generals could use woodland techniques, and North Americans could forget to do so.

The battle of Lake George was not over yet, not even after an unprofitable exchange of fire between Johnson's entrenched men and Dieskau's inadequate attacking force. Dieskau was wounded and captured in this part of the day's contest. His men were to find that day, September 8, 1755, very long, for late in the day as they attempted to regroup after the second engagement, they were attacked by 200 militiamen from Fort Edward. The three encounters, collectively known as the Battle of Lake George, cost 262 American casualties as compared to 230 of their opponents. The American frontiersmen had won in the defence of a makeshift fort after falling into a trap because of inadequate scouting. They had won the site of Fort William Henry and had closed the no-man's-land between opposing forts by fifteen miles; by the end of the year Governor Vaudreuil would finish this process by building Fort Carillon at the other end of Lake George.

Johnson's army did not fire a shot on Fort St. Frédéric, although the pace of the expedition's progress had been set by the cumbersome cannon intended for that purpose. Substantial forts could only be taken with a fairly large striking force, too large to live off the land, and with large cannon, too heavy to be moved without roads. The American militia and rangers, as well as their Iroquois allies, were being forced to plan, to move, and to think like regulars. General Dieskau's ambush is a reminder that at Lake George, as at Fort Necessity the previous year, it was not certain which conventions of war applied, those of a guerilla or those of a grenadier.

FORT BEAUSÉJOUR

Nova Scotia was the weakest British possession in North America in 1755. Louisbourg was not yet matched by Halifax (founded 1749) and the French had emphasized their interpretation of where Nova Scotia ended by building Forts Beauséjour and Gaspereau on the isthmus of Chignecto. Beauséjour was a very substantial fortress that defended winter communications between Louisbourg and Quebec, and stood as a sign of French interest and concern for the Acadians.

French forts on Nova Scotia's flank were one of its military weaknesses; the Acadians were the other. For forty years after the Peace of Utrecht the British government had compromised when the Acadians refused to take an unqualified oath of allegiance to the King of England. In 1753, the British Board of Trade advised the governor of Nova Scotia:

> The bringing of the French inhabitants to take the oath is certainly a very desirable thing, and the sooner they are brought to it the better; but it would be highly imprudent to disgust them by forcing it upon them at an improper time, and when they are quiet and at peace.[10]

If one asks what time would be proper, if not a time of peace and quiet, the dilemma of the British is apparent. For forty years British resolve to force the Acadians to submit or leave had always been broken by the argument that it was better for

Britain to have poor subjects than that Louisbourg or Canada should have better ones.

Charles Lawrence was a major in the British army. He had been in charge of an expedition to Chignecto that built Fort Lawrence (1749) as a rather light counterweight to Beauséjour. There he had fought Canadians, Acadians, Abenaquis and Micmacs in small engagements. As Lieutenant-Governor of Nova Scotia after 1753, he and his friend William Shirley worked out a plan to rid Chignecto of the French influence by capturing the two French forts. The plan became a reality as the third part of the 1755 campaign.

Some 2,000 New England volunteers and 285 British regulars were led by Colonel Robert Monckton of the Halifax garrison. With a good deal of traitorous assistance from a French officer, Thomas Pichon, Fort Beauséjour fell before the siege had more than begun; Fort Gaspereau capitulated without a shot being fired. This most successful and least arduous operation of 1755 was financed and led by Britain and manned largely by untrained New Englanders.

Military success was, however, followed by a drastic measure that was an admission of political failure—the expulsion of the Acadians. With the French forts in his possession and the struggle with France growing, Lieutenant-Governor Lawrence was determined to impose an unconditional oath on the Acadians. The Acadians had seen this kind of blustering by many a conscientious governor before, and had also seen these governors succumb to Acadian resolve not to bear arms against the French. In this instance, however the deadlock was resolved when Lawrence ordered Monckton's force to oversee the expulsion of Acadians unwilling to take the oath.

Expulsion was not a part of European war in the eighteenth century,[11] though there were refugees aplenty. Yet, the Canadian authorities themselves had threatened the Acadians in 1751 with expulsion if they failed to take an oath of allegiance to the King of France and join his militia.[12] It might also be argued that the expulsion was less brutal in the context of the guerilla war, which probably gave Lieutenant-Governor Lawrence the very jaundiced view that all Acadians would act like those he fought on the isthmus. Lawrence's actions were certainly not condemned by the British authorities; he was promoted to Governor of Nova Scotia late in 1755, a post that he held until his death in 1760, and he was made a brigadier-general in 1757. By the military measures of 1755 England conquered Acadia, but not the Acadians. The "solution" imposed on the Acadians, the first French wards of the British crown in North America, would encourage Canadians to fight even harder in the next five years.

* * *

In 1755, on balance, it could almost be said that Americans fought and Britain paid. The four major operations undertaken by Britain and America involved some 11,000 men, about 9,400 of them being American recruits into British regiments, American militiamen or volunteers, or American Indians. Britain assumed all the expenses of the two longest and most arduous expeditions — those of Braddock and Shirley — amounting to £120,000.[13] Robert Monckton's expedition was almost entirely manned by colonials, but it was entirely financed by Britain.[14] Although colonial assemblies paid all expenses connected with the Fort St. Frédéric operation, Britain granted them "a bounty and recompense" of £120,000 in 1756.[15] In addition to paying expenses, British funds paid the salaries of 6,000 of the 11,000 men in the field and, of course, Boscawen's fleet and other parts of the naval defence of North America were British expenses as well.

What was learned from 1755? The Duke of Cumberland, leader of the British army, younger son of the King and the leading figure in the oversight of the army in America in 1756, drew up a "Sketch for Next Year's Campaign in North America. Septr. 6, 1755." The base of operations was to be shifted to Albany, New York. One thousand British regulars were to supplement those in the colonies. Cumberland also wanted a British commander-in-chief:

> . . . sent over as soon as can be, to consult with the several Governors and jointly to concert measures with them, that he may not meet with those unforseen and unexpected Retardments, which delayed our Troops so long this last Spring.[16]

Lord Loudoun, Cumberland's choice as commander-in-chief, did not reach New York until July 23, 1756. The delay was due to changes of plans resulting from the sad news of Shirley's failure in New York. To avoid a repeat of some of Shirley's difficulties, Lord Loudoun's powers as commander-in-chief were greater than Braddock's or Shirley's. In addition, all provisions and supply of British and American troops were to be centred in Britain, rather than be subject to political pressures from colonial assemblies.[17] In 1756 there was also an increase in the number of regular troops in America. Instead of 1,000 British soldiers there were 2,000, and four battalions (4,000 men) of American regulars, the Royal Americans, were to be raised in the colonies and led by European officers.

What made the British government increase the role of regulars in 1756? The only successful expedition of 1755 was composed largely of New England volunteers, and the army that was destroyed under Braddock contained more regular soldiers than did the other three forces. Peter Wraxall, William Johnson's secretary in Indian negotiations, a Captain in the permanent garrison at New York, and a member of Johnson's army sent against Fort St. Frédéric, wrote to the British Secretary of State Henry Fox about this army:

> The Officers of this Army with a very few Exceptions are utter Strangers to Military Life and most of them in no Respect superior to the Men they are put over, They are like the heads and indeed are the heads of a Mob. The Men are raw Country Men. They are flattered with an easy & a speedy Conquest; All Arts are used to hide future Difficulties and Dangers from them, and the whole Undertaking in all it's Circumstances smoothed over to their Imaginations, . . .[18]

The difficulties in commanding "provincials" make expanded use of British regulars and the introduction of regular battalions of Americans under army discipline seem understandable. Putting European officers in charge of the American regulars was also in keeping with opinions like those of Wraxall, and could also be supported by the success of Monckton's command over Americans. Undoubtedly, the increased commitment of regulars owed something to the pride and prejudices of the British Army, anxious to vindicate itself for the preceding year's failures.

The four parts of Braddock's offensive, which seemed so similar in plan, proved different enough in execution to limit meaningful comparisons. Of four projected sieges only one materialized, and that one was no real test of organization or prowess. In three encounters between enemies, Monckton's attack on Fort Beauséjour was the only one that saw both sides accepting European conventions of war; the result was, perhaps by coincidence, the only Anglo-American victory. In this victory, British regulars were joined with New Englanders, and the men of New England were the only Americans who had conducted siege warfare, however unconventionally, against Acadia and Louisbourg. One thing the four expeditions did show. Most American recruits or militiamen, even colonial rangers and some Indians, seemed able to accept both the ends and the means of warfare as outlined by Braddock and the British government. After imposing the objectives of conventional war, the British government had little trouble convincing itself that those with experience and training in European warfare were better at it than those without.

Regardless of how much effort and reflection was required in planning the next Anglo-American campaign, the reconsiderations and changes took too long. Delays in reorganization helped the Franco-Canadian forces to take the offensive in 1756, and they would keep it for two years.

Chapter 5

Vaudreuil's Offensive, 1756-1757

The marquis de Vaudreuil, vain and self-important, was as proud of the fighting capacity of his fellow Canadians as he was of himself. He lost no opportunity to impress upon the French ministry how important he, and the Canadians, were in the successes of 1756 to 1757.[1]

As the survivors of Braddock's disaster made their way east under Colonel Dunbar, the frontier settlements of Pennsylvania, Maryland and Virginia received an unprecedented visitation of terror. By the spring of 1756 it was estimated that raids by Canadians and Indians, organized by Captain Dumas, the victor at the Monongahela, had resulted in 700 deaths or captures.[2] By the end of the summer these operations had spread to Carolina:

> All these provinces are laid waste for forty leagues [about 125 miles] from the foot of the mountains, in the direction of the sea. The number of prisoners in these territories since last April, is estimated at about three thousand—men, women and children, in addition to thirteen hundred horses carried off to the River Oyo, [Ohio] or the Beautiful river; the houses and barns that have been burnt, and the oxen and cows which have been killed wherever found, have not been counted.[3]

More than 2,000 men—Indians and Canadians—were involved in these raids. It is significant that no attack was launched upon Fort Cumberland, although parties raided nearly 200 miles beyond this isolated strongpoint. If these 2,000 men had constituted a single strike force, their supplies would have been

Pierre de Rigaud, marquis de Vaudreuil.

bulky enough to require control of a route past Fort Cumberland and, therefore, control of the fort itself. However, these men did not operate as a single force but rather as small bands of guerillas moving quickly and quietly through rough country, and hunting instead of carting supplies.

As a result of the terror caused by the Canadian guerilla bands, Virginia and Maryland were forced to defend their frontiers, and therefore stayed out of the war to the north until 1758. The militia of Virginia, led by Washington, attempted to stop the raids which, as well as being ferocious in themselves, had raised fears of slave uprisings.[4] But Virginia and Maryland were not free of the terror until Fort Duquesne fell in 1758.

While the raids took Virginia and Maryland out of the war, they put Pennsylvania in. Quaker assemblymen there, who could point to the colony's enlightened Indian policy as the colony's best defence throughout its seventy-five-year existence, now were forced to accept that Braddock's expedition had prompted counterattacks against the frontiersmen of Pennsylvania, as well as those of neighbouring colonies. Some Quaker assemblymen abandoned office rather than abandon passivism; but Pennsylvania went to war.[5]

Louis-Joseph, marquis de Montcalm.

OSWEGO, 1756

If the raids on the Southern American colonies represent the successful application of frontier warfare in all its ferocity, the Oswego campaign of 1756 shows the value of those tactics as an adjunct to European-style siege warfare in American conditions. During the winter of 1755/56 two Canadian scouting parties were sent to Oswego. Each returned with two prisoners for Vaudreuil to question. The second party also succeeded in destroying a fleet of more than sixty transport boats,[6] an important part of the supply system for Oswego. At the end of March, 1756, a force of about 400 men—Canadians, Indians and 60 regulars—trekked on snowshoes more than 200 miles to attack and destroy Fort Bull, which defended the portage between the Mohawk and Oswego rivers. The eighty-man garrison was slaughtered after the fort was stormed; gunpowder, ammunition and provisions were destroyed, as were horses, wagons and boats.[7] At the beginning of July a stronger force of 900 men struck at the same place, this time attacking and destroying a convoy of some 300 supply boats, and killing more than fifty of a force of 500 Americans in the convoy.[8] The attackers lost only four men. These attacks on communication lines added to the miserable condition of the American garrison at Oswego, and the reconnaisance parties gathered information helpful in planning the siege. In fact, a preliminary siege net was around Oswego for more than six months.

Like many North American forts, Oswego began as a trading post and, therefore, was situated at the edge of the mouth of the Oswego River. The fortifications were expanded with the Anglo-French struggle, but the fort was still in a river valley commanded by higher ground on both sides. In the year before the siege, the main fort, now called Fort George, had been further strengthened and subsidiary forts had been built on the high ground—Fort Ontario to the north and Fort Oswego to the south.[9] But three weak forts did not make a strong one. The troublesome transfer of authority from Governor Shirley to the new commander-in-chief, Lord Loudoun, resulted in increased signs that the garrison of some 1,800 Americans had been forgotten. Oswego, a prime objective for Vaudreuil, seemed ready for the taking. Montcalm's legitimate suspicions of the concentration of the British force on the Hudson for a push north seemed an additional reason to hit Oswego and draw some of this manpower westward up the Mohawk.

The siege of Oswego, like the year's offensive, was an effective combination of the techniques of Old World and New. Montcalm's force included only 1,300 *troupes de terre,* " . . . the remainder, soldiers of the Colony [*troupes de la marine*], Militiamen and Indians."[10] Vaudreuil assigned his audacious if not reckless brother, François-Pierre de Rigaud de Vaudreuil, and a force of 1,500 Canadians and Indians as the vanguard of Montcalm's 3,000-man army. This vanguard surrounded Fort Ontario on the morning of August 11, and three mornings later they led the way across the Oswego River to isolate and harass Fort George. More of Montcalm's cannon came to bear on Fort George during that morning, and the menacing sound of Indian warriors grew in intensity. When the commander of the garrison was killed, the morale of the garrison disappeared, and the white flag was run up before noon.[11] Montcalm remarked:

> It is to be concluded that the English, when transplanted, are no longer like those in Europe. We must look at my Lord Loudoun's Scotchmen, for it appears that General has arrived [from Britain]. . . .[12]

Montcalm was also aware that Canadians were not Frenchmen, and Vaudreuil's kind of war was not his. He wrote the minister of war:

> My whole conduct on that occasion, [Oswego] and the arrangements I had concluded on, in the face of eighteen hundred men, are so utterly at variance with ordinary rules, that the audacity with which that expedition has been executed, must be considered rashness in Europe. Therefore, I beseech you, my Lord, as a particular favour, to assure his Majesty, should he ever, as I hope he will, employ me in his armies, that I shall conduct myself on different principles.[13]

Montcalm went from the success on Lake Ontario to spend an uneasy autumn on Lake Champlain at the new Fort Carillon. The Oswego offensive had been so successful and swift that it had failed to draw any reinforcements from Lord Loudoun's camp at Albany. Though Montcalm had a force of more than 5,000 men at Carillon, and 2,000 more could be called upon from Montreal, he had cause to be nervous at the end of September. Not only was it feared that Loudoun could march 10,000 men on twenty-four hours' notice and raise a force of 20,000, but Loudoun would have the advantage of water transport on the Hudson for a full month after navigation ceased on the Richelieu. By contrast, it would be at least a three days' march for any reinforcements that came down from Montreal. Even if Loudoun decided that it was too late to attack, there was a long hungry winter in store, for the grain crop had failed. Beyond this, there was the danger of an attack in the spring, when the Hudson would again be free of ice before the Richelieu.[14] Despite these apprehensions, there was no offensive from the south that autumn or the next spring.

The war of the woods and that of the battlefield had merged well in 1756, though there were signs that friendly rivalries between French and Canadians could deepen to enmity. Montcalm was a little uneasy with the Oswego campaign, and on November 1 he wrote the minister of war, in coded passages of a letter, several remarks on maltreatment by Vaudreuil, "a General who knows not how to speak of war. . . . M. de Vaudreuil wishes to besiege Fort George; difficult; that of Fort Lidius, impossible." He explained what he would like to do the following year—attack Acadia as another diversion from the build-up on the Hudson.[15] Vaudreuil did not tell the home minister what he planned to do, but begged for 1,800 men and provisions:

> I suppose, in these propositions, that the Court of England will not send over additional forces to New England. Should it decide upon sending any, you will no doubt know it, and in such case I beg you to be pleased to add to my requisitions a second complement of troops in proportion to that which will be sent by the English.[16]

A French ministerial assessment of the Canadian situation reveals the arguments (or sophistry) used to limit the reinforcement to 1,800 men, even though it was known that England was about to send 8,000 regulars to America. After arguing that maintenance of the successful offensive was ideal, the ministry suggested that a defensive focus would be most appropriate for the next year. If this could be maintained for a year, a French squadron would be sent out in 1758 to help retake Acadia (Montcalm's plan). After giving very good reasons why the British force would be designed against either Louisbourg or Quebec, the ministry argued that Vaudreuil would not need troops for use against Lord Loudoun's force in New York. And what if the massive reinforcements were meant for Loudoun? In that case the Anglo-American offensive would focus on Fort St. Frédéric (what of Fort Carillon?) and the Franco-Canadian forces could be drawn from all fronts and successfully oppose Loudoun.

Perhaps the important reasons why more reinforcements were not sent were those mentioned after this crystal-ball gazing. Sufficient men-of-war could not be spared to convoy a more substantial fleet of transports. Annual expenses of the French government in Canada had risen sharply from 1,000,000 livre a year to as much as 8,000,000, and the accumulated debt of the "colonial chest" had reached some 14,000,0000 livre. Also, the Canadian wheat crop had failed, and more troops would require even larger supporting shipments of grain—more transportation difficulties and more expense.[17]

FORT WILLIAM HENRY, 1757

What Vaudreuil had done at Oswego in 1756, he attempted to do at Fort William Henry the following year.[18] Several circumstances, however, conspired to make the use of the 1756 strategy more difficult. First, Fort William Henry was not at the end of a long and tortuous communication line; it was only fifteen miles from the strong Fort Edward on the Hudson, and both could be reinforced speedily from Albany. Manpower could have meaning in this situation, and Lord Loudoun had the manpower. In the 1757 campaign there would be no flimsy forts with small garrisons like Fort Bull.[19] Second, grain shortages were severe and persistent. In a sense, the poor crops put Canada herself in a state of siege for the final four years of the struggle. In these circumstances any attempt to besiege a fort had to achieve quick success, or the besiegers would be hungrier than the besieged. Third, the rift between Montcalm and Governor Vaudreuil was widening. It did not help morale

Rigaud's winter attack on Fort William Henry, 1757—a nineteenth century conception.

or planning. If 1756 showed the marriage of European and frontier warfare, 1757 saw their divorce.

During the winter, Canadian scouting parties brought in information and prisoners,[20] from whom it became apparent that the preparation of a major offensive was under way at Fort William Henry, garrisoned by 500 British regulars.

Vaudreuil's first major move against Fort William Henry was subject to two interpretations in 1757, and the question remains unsolved. The Governor explained the raid led by his brother in late February and early March, 1757, as a preliminary to a siege. Rigaud led a force of 1,500 men (650 militiamen, 300 Indians, 300 *troupes de la marine,* and 250 French regulars) to the fort. Then:

> . . . in order to carry out my intentions, my brother was obliged to summon the enemy and, by his manoeuvers, to persuade him that he was about to scale the fort. This ruse had wonderful success.[21]

Under cover of this ruse, Rigaud's men succeeded in burning four "cruisers," several large longboats, 350 bateaux, wagons, a storehouse of provisions, arms and clothing, a sawmill, the hospital sheds as well as houses, timber for building boats, and firewood. With only five casualties:

> M. de Rigaud accomplished the important mission I had confided to him. He left nothing for me to desire in what I had prescribed to him.
> This event changes the situation of the Colony, and renders it, so to say, as advantageous as it was critical.[22]

The marquis de Montcalm saw the matter differently. He had submitted to Vaudreuil a plan ". . . of surprising Fort George [Fort William Henry], and burning, at least, the outer parts of the fort with 800 men. . . ."[23] He had asked that the leadership of the expedition be given to one of his French officers, M. de Bourlamarque. While admitting the significance of what was actually achieved, Montcalm left the impression with his ministerial correspondents that Rigaud's purpose had

104 ❖ *Guerillas and Grenadiers*

been to take the fort, and he should have been able to do it.[24] Montcalm also revealed the rivalry with Canadians:

> As we are not accustomed to such marches in Europe, and as the Canadians who are accustomed to brag, asserted that our troops could not support such fatigues, I paid particular attention carefully to select officers and soldiers qualified in every respect. Therefore were the Canadians forced to admit that we were not inferior to them in any point.[25]

Montcalm's imputations did not say that Rigaud attempted a siege and failed, but a third figure in the event, Lieutenant-Colonel William Eyre, British commander at Fort William Henry, did tell the story as that of a successful frustration of a siege.

What have the historians done with this evidence? Francis Parkman read Eyre, Montcalm and his subordinates on the matter, and his account makes the event appear very much like a British victory at a time when British victories were few.[26] Most Canadian writers have found Montcalm, perhaps understandably, more attractive than Vaudreuil or his brother, and therefore accept the view that the Canadian claims of success were a way of salvaging something from an attack that failed.[27] One recent writer supports Vaudreuil against Montcalm and sees Rigaud's raid in the context of Vaudreuil's repeating the strategy employed successfully against Oswego in 1756.[28] Vaudreuil did not give his brother written instructions, as far as is known, and even if a journal of a participant were discovered, which of Rigaud's men would not say it was a victory and which of Eyre's men would not say it was their success?

Whatever it was intended to be, Rigaud's raid contributed to, though by no means determined, the defensive posture of Fort William Henry as the 1757 campaign opened. Vaudreuil believed that, as a result of his brother's success, a Franco-Canadian initiative should be directed against Fort William Henry. This belief was supported by evidence that Lord Loudoun and much of his army were preoccupied with an intended expedition against Louisbourg. Both Vaudreuil and Montcalm were anxious to launch the offensive, but nothing could be done until provisions arrived from France.[29] By the middle of July few of the provisions and only a few of the reinforcements had arrived. The soldiers' rations had been reduced to a pound and a half of bread a day, and those of the citizens of Quebec to four ounces a day.[30] When 1,000 Indians arrived at Montreal to join an offensive, Vaudreuil was forced to do something, although a couple of weeks earlier he had written:

> Tis greatly to be desired that I be not obliged, before the receipt of these [French] provisions, to employ our forces to resist the enemy, for then I would be forced to seize the little that remains with each individual and farmer in the Colony, and to support the towns and villages on the domestic cattle, which would destroy the breed.[31]

Montcalm, in reporting the decision to act, says, "the Marquis de Vaudreuil finally determined to search up provisions among the farmers, which produced something, ..."[32] The campaign against Fort William Henry can only be understood if this shortage of food is kept in mind.

As Montcalm prepared to move south from Fort Carillon, two major preliminary skirmishes occurred. A party of 200 Canadians and Indians attacked the environs of Fort Edward, including a fifty-man guard for shipwrights. Montcalm reported to Vaudreuil that Lieutenant Marin, in charge of the raid, ". . . was unwilling to amuse himself making prisoners; he brought in only one, and 32 scalps, . . ."[33] More prisoners in this case could have been very useful for information, but the refusal to take prisoners suggests that the attackers were attempting to impress the garrison at Fort Edward by their ferocity.

The second, and more important, preliminary scheme was an ambush of the armed British barges patrolling Lake George. The Ottawas suggested the ambush and aided in carrying it out, accompanied by Canadians, under Rigaud, and French regulars. Twenty of the twenty-two barges were sunk or captured, 160 men were captured and an equal number killed or drowned.[34] This time prisoners were taken, because they could give information about the state of Fort William Henry. As a result of this action, the barges replacing the cruisers and bateaux, which Rigaud had destroyed earlier, were likewise out of the way.[35] Montcalm's siege train could now travel the length of the lake to the target fort without challenge.

After these preparations, Montcalm's army of 5,500 men[36]—regulars, militia and Indians—began a siege of Fort William Henry on August 3. The 2,400-man garrison under Colonel Munro justifiably felt deserted by General Webb, who had information, men, and time to reinforce the garrison, but failed to do so.[37] Munro capitulated on August 9, after receiving a captured letter from Webb that made it clear reinforcements were not coming.

It is no coincidence that the first thing Montcalm mentioned as taken at Fort William Henry was ". . . a heap of provisions for the subsistence of 6,000 men for six weeks . . ."[38]—the besiegers had set out with only ten days' provisions.[39] Then cannon and ammunition are mentioned next, then the garrison, ". . . which I should have made prisoners had the Colony had provision. The clause, not to serve during eighteen months, is of more advantage to it."[40] Though the Oswego garrison had been taken to Canada in 1756, there was not enough food for 2,400 unwelcome guests in 1757. Montcalm did what he saw as the only alternative—escort these 2,400 men to their nearest fort, Fort Edward, on their promise not to fight for eighteen months.

The curious civilities of European warfare were not at all appreciated by the Indians, and it is not surprising that—with or without the influence of rum—they harried and plundered the column of prisoners. They hatcheted those who resisted or fled to the woods and held 600—reduced to 200—prisoners for themselves, until persuaded to take them to Montreal. Perhaps it is not surprising that some Canadians did not help the unfortunate victims, nor that it was Montcalm and the French regulars who restored order eventually, after Montcalm offered to sacrifice himself in place of the British victims. It should not be surprising, either, that Vaudreuil gave the Indians a scolding and two barrels of brandy per prisoner when they arrived at Montreal. Something over thirty men had been killed in the "massacre,"* probably less than half the number of those killed at Fort Bull, the previous year, without so much as an offer of quarter. To allow a force nearly as large as Canada's assault force at Oswego in 1756 to march away fully-armed, and return to fight another day (General Abercromby absolved the army of its pledge not to fight, because of the "massacre"[41]) was not the Indian's idea of war. Had not Captain Dumas, at Fort Duquesne, encouraged them to kill defenceless settlers? Had not Canadians joined them in these raids and bragged of these as exploits? The Indians' understandable rebellion at Fort William Henry is the most unfortunate aspect of the mixture of the frontier and European standards of war with which the Franco-Canadians generally had success during 1754/57.

The Vaudreuil offensive ended in mid-August, earlier than Vaudreuil had wished. His orders to Montcalm were to go on from Fort William Henry to take Fort Edward, fifteen miles away on the Hudson. Montcalm refused the risk, and the campaign closed with both men writing damning letters home to the ministry.[42] Whether or not the stores captured at Fort William Henry could have sustained the offensive, shortage of provisions was a legitimate reason for Montcalm's concern that the Canadians get home to bring in the harvest.

There was a unity and plan to the Vaudreuil offensive, that is too easily lost by approaching the story of the year from the south and seeing it as a result of myriad Anglo-American mistakes. The limited resources available in Canada were used capably. Vaudreuil could see that with the build-up of English regulars, the maxim that "offence is the best defence" became "offence is the only defence." The last blow struck in 1757 was a raid late in November on German settlers in the Mohawk valley. Provisions bound for Albany were destroyed and about

---

*The figures range from Lanctôt's twenty-nine (III, 148) to Peckham's two hundred (p. 163). Gipson (*op. cit.*, VII, 87) says that the number "was probably not less than two hundred and may have greatly exceeded that number." Gipson also argues that the numbers were minimized by American reports for fear of terror it would inspire and the bad effect on recruiting. Parkman accepts the figure of about fifty (*Wolfe and Montcalm*, I, 512). Lanctôt's argument that this did not constitute a massacre is true enough, but the colonial press could make a "massacre" out of the death of five persons in the 1770's.

fifty people were killed.[43] It may be wondered whether this raid fits the pattern as part of some offensive design for 1758, but it seems unlikely. The comment that this raid destroyed "in grain, of all sorts, a much larger quantity than the Island of Montreal has produced in years of abundance. The same of hogs,"[44] seems almost pathetic in itself, or as justification for the raid. These provisions meant a great deal more to the Canadians than they meant to the British army, which could draw from all the American colonies as well as any sources across the Atlantic. Such terrorism would force Virginia, Pennsylvania or Maryland to deflect more resources to frontier defence, but the British forces assembled on the Hudson were not paid for by colonial taxpayers. This army could, and would, focus its offensive directly on Canada, even if American colonists clamoured for protection against frontier raids. Vaudreuil could see, at least as early as August of 1757, that he would be forced on the defensive in 1758,[45] yet he favoured an aggressive defence to the end.

A year later, after Montcalm's successful defence of Fort Carillon, the General submitted several papers on defence to Vaudreuil. One of these began:

> It is no longer the time when a few scalps, or the burning [of] a few houses is any advantage or even an object. Petty means, petty ideas, petty Councils about details are now dangerous, and waste material and time; circumstances exact determined and decisive measures. The war is entirely changed in this part of the world according to the manner the English are attacking us; nothing less is at stake than the utter and impending loss of the Colony or its salvation, that is to say, the postponement of its fall.[46]

By this time Montcalm was advocating retreat from the Ohio, from Lake Ontario and from Lake Champlain, and the concentration on the defence of Quebec and Montreal.

Vaudreuil insisted:

> 'Tis for the true and most solid interest of the Colony, that I essentially adhere to contesting the ground on our frontiers inch by inch with the enemy, whilst M. de Montcalm has made it appear that the troops of the line wish only to

preserve their reputation and return to France without having experienced a single check; they think more seriously of their private interests than of the safety of Canada.[47]

When the French ministry imposed the defensive strategy by putting Montcalm over Vaudreuil in military matters, in February, 1759,[48] the Vaudreuil offensive was formally ended, though it had petered out by the end of 1757. It is doubtful that continuation of Vaudreuil's policy could have made any difference in 1759—the siege of Canada, which was tightening from 1757, was hampering enough, and the British troops, some 23,000 strong, had an overwhelming advantage. Indeed, once the British Navy had stopped almost all aid from France, the old odds of twenty to one became the impossible odds of one hundred to one. Perhaps a realist would have reduced the contest to a duel for a citadel from the start, but a partisan could not. The offensives of 1756 and 1757 might not have been taken by a realist, for the cry to abandon the castle and defend the keep were nearly as valid then. Whether or not he could have saved the colony, Vaudreuil's policy certainly postponed its fall. By accepting the defence strategy of Montcalm, did France doom Canada? By fighting to suit regular troops, were militiamen, who could not be transformed into troops of the line, made less effective?

Chapter 6

Pitt's Offensive, 1758-1760

William Pitt the elder, Britain's Secretary of State, was an eloquent patriot and a firm believer in himself. In the eloquence possible in parliamentary opposition he was a master of bombast and ridicule, making charges based on limited evidence, and creating stirring phrases that would come back to haunt him once he had achieved political power himself. Inconsistency, the failure to be true to oneself, is a charge historians are still keen to level when other questions of how to judge men in their own time become difficult. Yet, it can often be nothing more than accusing a grown man of learning something. In the case of Pitt, politics were involved, but he also learned.

As self-styled saviour of the British Empire, Pitt had many supporters, but few friends. When he achieved real power in the summer of 1757, a political opponent commented acidly that Pitt "wanted friends for places, more than places for his friends."[1] His chief colleagues, the Duke of Newcastle and the Earl of Hardwicke, were not his friends, and they, like the King, only worked with Pitt of necessity. The King's younger son, the Duke of Cumberland, who was Captain-General of the British army, had made Pitt's dismissal a precondition of leading an army on the continent in the spring of 1757. In judging military men Pitt was as erratic as in most other things. Yet as a leader of a nation suffering defeat he was an inspiration to the populace, an assurance to merchants, and to the armed forces a determined warrior who could make the nation pay enough to win.

Pitt's power was achieved and strengthened by the military disasters that befell British armies in 1757. The Duke of Cumberland would withdraw from public life after his campaign ended in the Convention of Kloster-Zeven, which his

William Pitt, English Secretary of State for the Southern Department (1756-57, 1757-61). This engraving is from a portrait done in 1753, when Pitt was 45.

father repudiated. Vaudreuil's successes in 1756 and 1757 could easily be interpreted as Lord Loudoun's failures, and this close friend and follower of Cumberland would be eased out of his job just when he was making the transition to the kind of war demanded of him in North America. The ousting of Cumberland and Loudoun not only meant new men, but the positions became less responsible as the aggressive Secretary of State drew more of the military power to himself. Pitt had some acquaintance with, and interest in, military matters before military success became his political *raison d'être*. In the successor to Cumberland, Lord Ligonier, Pitt found an able and experienced professional assistant whose ideas would often become Pitt's ideas. Yet, with the British distrust of the army, Pitt was able to impose civilian control and also monopolize the credit, or blame, for the strategy employed.[2]

In replacing Lord Loudoun as commander-in-chief in North America, Pitt all but destroyed that position. Loudoun had possessed more powers than his predecessor, Braddock, powers that had encouraged united military action on the part of the English colonies. But now not only did Pitt assume negotiations with colonial authorities rather than leaving this to the new commander-in-chief, General James Abercromby, but he also gave the commander-in-chief less room for initiative by issuing extensive instructions and giving independent commands to Generals Amherst and Forbes in America.[3] In fact, by the end of 1757 the detailed British planning of the North American war had migrated across the Atlantic to London, as much as six months away by exchange of letters.

RENEWED OFFENSIVE, 1758

In 1755 the Anglo-American offensive had been diffused to include attacks on Forts Beauséjour, St. Frédéric, Niagara and Duquesne. Though the strategy had been designed to remove the French from what planners assumed to be British territory, success came in only one of these efforts. In 1758, when limited war in America was a thing of the past,* the British offensive

*One English writer with experience in Virginia wrote in 1757: "If you would root the French out of America altogether indeed, take Crown Point, Montreal and Quebec; which may not be so easily done perhaps, nor so much for our purpose. But if you would recover your losses, secure yourselves, and prevent the farther progress of the French, or their future encroachments, take Niagara and Fort Duquesne. This we apprehend might not be so difficult to do, as to attack Canada, whilst it would do all that we want." John Mitchell, *The Contest in America* . . . (London, 1757), p. 52.

featured attacks in the same four localities as in 1755. Action was taken against Louisbourg in the east, Fort Carillon on Lake Champlain, Fort Frontenac on Lake Ontario, and Fort Duquesne. Why not focus on one or two overpowering thrusts aimed at conquest?

Lord Loudoun's plan of operations for 1758 had involved these four operations. Pitt would make alterations in manpower used, but Loudoun's plan was carried out. Pitt dropped the Lake Ontario offensive, only to find that it was carried out successfully on colonial initiative. Loudoun and Pitt had no choice about the Louisbourg attempt. A siege of the fortress in 1757 failed prematurely, but left an army wintering at Halifax. Loudoun would have reinforced this group with Americans, who would have been valuable in road building and similar work; Pitt made the 1758 siege almost exclusively the work of British regulars.[4] Loudoun had planned a simultaneous two-pronged attack aimed at Montreal. One attack, by way of Fort Frontenac, would have drawn defenders from the Canadian Lake Champlain forts. These forts would then have received the other attack by a force predominantly composed of British regulars, who could have been put into action earlier than colonial forces. Pitt dropped the Fort Frontenac expedition (though Abercromby approved its execution after his attempt on Fort Carillon failed) and reduced the proportion of regulars in the army on the Lake George frontier. Pitt's tamperings with the plans regarding Fort Duquesne brought costly delays, but no major change in this operation. In its intention to relieve pressure on the frontiers of the southern colonies, increasingly manned by regular troops,[5] to carry the war to the enemy on the Lake George front, and to gain something from the previous year's efforts against Louisbourg, the campaign plan of 1758 was similar to that of 1755.

Why did Pitt's offensive of 1758 succeed in three of its four objectives, whereas the 1755 offensive had failed in three of its four assignments? There is no simple answer, but before discussing the British operations of 1758, it is worthwhile to point out some general changes that had occurred. Whereas one in seven of the 11,000 fighting men in the 1755 campaign was a British regular, more than half of the men involved in the 1758 offensive were British soldiers. The reasons for this change ranged all the way from the prejudices of regular officers against colonials, to the inability of British recruiting officers to compete with the bounties offered by colonial governments for men who were often held for defence of their own colonies. Though the vital function of the colonial rangers was readily recognized, the American militia was not highly regarded by the British. British regulars were cheaper, more reliable under fire and, if they had spent the winter in the New World, they could be moved to the attack before colonial levies could be recruited, mustered and moved.[6] There is no doubt that, in their enthusiasm to put British regulars on the line, British officers often overlooked the advantage of some American support services. If Americans fought and Britain paid in 1755, by 1758 Britain was doing much more of the fighting and paying more.

The Royal Navy, like the British army, was more heavily committed to the New World offensive in 1758 than had been possible in 1755. The fleet that brought the regulars to America also brought its own gunpower and manpower and, as the offensive on the North Atlantic focused on the bases of Louisbourg and Quebec, the fleet's role increased tremendously. Also, 1757 had seen the last major "escapes" of French support squadrons for Canada; the increasing effect of the naval net laid from Plymouth to Gibraltar was visible in 1758.

Money fights even more than it talks, and Pitt sold Britain a very expensive war. He did not win a European war in America nor, as he once said, an American war in Germany—he greatly increased Britain's commitment to both wars. In 1757 he had helped to limit Britain's support of Hanover, thereby keeping the Anglo-Hanoverian army on the defensive to avoid the impression that it was defending Prussia's western frontiers. This policy was disastrous. In 1758 Prussia was granted a subsidy, and the budget of the revived Anglo-Hanoverian army increased seven-fold over that of 1757. The bill for fighting in the New World went up sharply, too. Pitt introduced a true requisitioning system for colonial assistance. With full reimbursement for all expenses, colonial assemblies were more than anxious to earn sterling by prompt, and expensive, provision of men, supplies, or services. Colonial governments would come out of the war in better financial condition than they went in. Britain's reimbursements would amount to £866,666.[7] Money could make even the cumbersome and awkward structure of the first British empire yield results. More men, more ships, and more money were, then, the advantages of the British forces that attempted to do a better job of the sort attempted by the British in 1755.

Louisbourg   Louisbourg would not fall as easily in 1758 as it had to the New Englanders in 1745. The shore of Gabarus Bay, where the earlier invaders had landed, were now protected by a line of entrenchments that would make landing forces suffer tremendously. The strength that Louisbourg could have, and the effort France was willing to make to defend it, had been illustrated in 1757. Lord Loudoun, and his patron the Duke of Cumberland, had favoured an assault upon Quebec as a means of breaking what could well have been a deadlock if the Lake Champlain frontier remained the focal point of the struggle. Pitt wanted to see Louisbourg taken before any attempt was made at Quebec, but he left the decision, and the onus, with Loudoun. By mid-July, 1757, he had a force of nearly 15,000 men and a fleet of seventeen ships of the line, with a similar number of minor support vessels, in addition to transports.[8] Despite all this military might, amounting to more than four times the force sent to the same destinations in 1745, Loudoun decided that it was unwise to attack Louisbourg. What could stop a force like that? Perhaps the cream of the French navy could. Eighteen ships of the line, constituting the most powerful fleet ever gathered in the New World,[9] were assembled in Louisbourg harbour before the end of June, 1757. Three small French squadrons had escaped the British navy and by daring and devious means gathered at Louisbourg under Admiral de la Motte. This fleet did not come out to meet Loudoun, and Loudoun decided not to try Louisbourg that year. Both men were treated by their governments as though they had acted like cowards, though both can be defended.

In 1758, however, Louisbourg did not have a huge French fleet. British blockades in the Mediterranean and Bay of Biscay kept all but six ships from reaching Louisbourg—these could not stop the impending blow, and did not even escape it.

The British assault landing at Louisbourg's Gabarus Bay on June 8, 1758, was the first of a kind. Without protection of a fleet, Louisbourg itself could not long stand a determined siege.* The real defence of Louisbourg occurred at the shoreline of the bay, west of the harbour, which provided the only landing place for an attacking force intent on dragging cannon to Louisbourg. The shoreline was prepared almost as an outwork of the fortress, with thirty cannon mounted at strategic places along the shore to the west of the harbour and more than 2,300 regular troops entrenched behind a twenty-foot *abatis*.[10] (An *abatis* was an eighteenth century version of barbed wire, an entanglement of freshly-cut trees with sharpened branches to greet the enemy. Too green to light, too entangled to move, this barrier could ruin a conventional frontal attack.)

The British were well aware of the entrenchments at Gabarus Bay and, therefore, considered a landing to the north of Louisbourg and also prepared to storm the beaches of Gabarus Bay. As the troops waited at Halifax for General Amherst and the fleet in the spring of 1758, practice landings from ships' boats were repeated. The helpless minutes when soldiers waded from the boats to the beach were reduced, and the number of troops landed at one time was increased.[11] If the 1745 landing had allowed a maximum of separation between the landing force and the fleet, the 1758 attempt demanded a maximum of cooperation. When the real test came, heavy swells postponed the landing and hampered it when attempted. The practice landings had not included enemy cannon and musket fire. Brigadier-General James Wolfe, a hard-driving young leader of the assault, seems to have called it off as madness. But then he noticed that a boatload of infantrymen had found a "neck of rocks" which allowed them to land safe from French fire. Though gaining the height was to be achieved by a fierce bayonet charge, nothing would have been possible save for this bit of good fortune, and Wolfe's prompt use of it.[12]

Once the 13,000-man British army was ashore and the surprised and confused defenders of the outworks had successfully retreated to the fort, the heroics were with the defenders.

*Perhaps this fact had made it easier for the British to return Louisbourg to France in 1748.

Governor Augustin de Drucour's defence force was outnumbered three to one by an army intent on taking Louisbourg and Quebec in one season. With dogged courage, in the face of appeals from the residents, mounting losses, and limited supplies, Drucour held out until the end of July. Major-General Jeffrey Amherst, said by one historian of the British army to be "the greatest military administrator produced by England since the death of Marlborough, and remained the greatest until the rise of Wellington,"[13] conducted a thorough but unimaginative attack that contributed to the length of the siege, and the length of the struggle for Canada. Drucour had kept Amherst from Quebec.

Fort Carillon (Ticonderoga) Fort Carillon was Montcalm's victory; it was as much a victory over Governor Vaudreuil as it was a success over Major-General James Abercromby. The feud between the Governor and Montcalm had grown from bickering in 1756 to deep-rooted hostility by 1758.[14] Conflict over strategy and mutual distrust might have cost much more than it did, but it goes far to explain why Montcalm had no more than 3,500 men when he was attacked by a force of 15,000.

The defence of Fort Carillon was the clearest, and most successful, demonstration of Montcalm's defensive strategy. Though the fort was less than three years old, Montcalm's engineer-in-chief assured him, in concluding a report on the fort, "Were I entrusted with the siege of it, I should require only six mortar and two cannon."*[15] Montcalm could not, therefore, trust the fort, and instead of using it to defend his army, he positioned the army to defend the fort. Entrenchments were dug across the only path of direct assault on the fort, and one-quarter of a mile from it. Earth from the trenches, logs and sandbags completed this phase of the defenceworks on a crest bounded by a river on one side and a forest and ravine on the other. Beyond the trenches the troops worked feverishly on

---

*The two cannon, doubtless, would have been placed on what was later named Mount Defiance, to the south of the fort. Unlike many other forts, Carillon was not a fortified trading post with that excuse for its positioning. Yet the fort was well located to stop smaller, water-bound expeditions and its lakeside site facilitated reinforcement and supply (as Lévis' arrival indicates) as well as orderly retreat.

July 7, 1758, to complete an *abatis*. While major scouting parties were sent out to give token resistance to the advancing enemy and gather information, all encounters were accidental, and the advance forces were given orders to drop back within the defence works as the enemy approached. Here was Montcalm's overall strategy for Canada operating in miniature. Montcalm was fortunate that the attack was precisely the kind for which he was best prepared.

Major-General Abercromby has been held responsible by most English-speaking historians for what happened at Fort Carillon, while French-speaking historians often emphasize Montcalm's contribution to that battle. In most people's eyes, Montcalm needs no defence—he won against odds of more than four to one; that is defence enough. However, the grossly inflated accounts of British casualties that Montcalm and his lieutenants sent home—stories of 3,000 instead of 550 killed—helped to cement the glory of that day and strengthen Montcalm and the French position against Vaudreuil and the Canadian one.[16]

On the other side of that day's battle, few have given Abercromby more than blame. A colonial captain fumed that use of cannon on the hill dominating Fort Carillon

> ... must have occur'd to any blockhead who was not absolutely so far sunk in Idiotism as to be oblig'd to wear a bib and bells.[17]

A modern military historian has claimed that Abercromby had three alternatives to the frontal attack. First, he could have attacked from the flanks. This would have meant approaching from the woods and ravine on the French right, an alternative impossible if regular troops were to engage in battle, and Abercromby held the prevailing prejudice against colonial troops. Second, artillery could have been used against the breastworks. This is true if it is assumed that there was time, but was there? Abercromby had been told that 3,000 men were coming in to reinforce 6,000 troops under Montcalm. All prisoners taken before the battle by the British seemed to agree on this lie, but should Abercromby be blamed for believing it? Lévis had an independent command of 3,800 men originally designed for an attack in western New York. How was Abercromby to know that only 400, not 3,000, of these would be sent as reinforcements by the spiteful Vaudreuil? It was not primarily the strangely unanimous story told by French prisoners that made Abercromby hurry. Lieutenant Matthew Clark reconnoitred the French defences from Mount Defiance and reported that they could be taken, since they were not yet completed. Abercromby was guilty primarily in persisting with the frontal attack after the first encounters proved how mistaken Clark had been.

The third alternative for Abercromby, which F. W. Fortescue suggests, was ". . . to mask this improvised stronghold with a part of his force and push on with the rest northward up Lake Champlain and so cut off at once Montcalm's supplies and his retreat."[18] This suggestion, which Fortescue thinks would have been the best alternative, is based upon two assumptions: first, that Montcalm had only 3,500 men (which was true) and not the 6,000 that Abercromby expected to meet; second, that there was no chance that it could be Abercromby's supply lines that would be severed, not Montcalm's. There would be very few European generals willing to advance with an enemy stronghold on his own supply lines. This strategy might have value if the primary reason for haste was to stop reinforcements from arriving at Fort Carillon. If, on the other hand, the primary reason for haste was the report of Lieutenant Clark that the French breastworks were not yet complete, "masking" would only allow them to be finished. From hindsight, we can be certain that Abercromby should have waited a few hours to make use of cannon, or even a few days so that the *abatis* could have been set afire easily. Yet Abercromby, while certainly not brilliant or imaginative, need not have been a candidate for "bib and bells" to do what he did. Guy Frégault would go even further in demolishing the magnitude of Montcalm's success by arguing that the English colonials were little more than observers at this battle, as casualty rates suggest. If this is accepted, no European general would have considered it ignominious for 7,000 men to fail in assaulting an entrenched force of half that number.[19] This is not the only place where sweeping condemnations come

120 ❖ *Guerillas and Grenadiers*

easiest from ignorance, and stick easiest to the perennial victim of history, the loser.

Fort Frontenac Compared to Shirley's Niagara campaign of three years earlier, Lieutenant-Colonel John Bradstreet's attack on Fort Frontenac was extremely successful. Abercromby was reluctant to go against his instructions from Pitt in order to let Bradstreet go on his venture. There were difficulties in getting wagons, too, but these were minor in comparison with Shirley's problems. The forces under Bradstreet were similar to Shirley's, overwhelmingly colonials in British pay, without many Indians. Bradstreet had 157 regulars and a total force about 500 stronger than Shirley's. Bradstreet made much better time in arriving at Oswego, and maintenance of secrecy was unusually good. "Even the commanding officers of corps were uncertain, at leaving the Oneida station, whether they were to be led against Niagara, Osmegatchie [Oswegatchie] or Cadaraqui."[20] That the last of these, Fort Frontenac, was the objective was undoubtedly an additional advantage of Bradstreet over Shirley. Shirley had not been authorized to attack the accepted French possession of Fort Frontenac in 1755, when France and Britain were at peace. While Fort Frontenac's strength prevented Shirley from sailing from Oswego to attack the diplomatically acceptable target of Fort Niagara (see above, p. 90), Fort Frontenac itself could be isolated by a surprise attack, particularly in its weakened state in 1758. Bradstreet's army was neither temperamentally nor logistically capable of besieging a fortress for long. With entrenching tools, ammunition and provisions in short supply, the besiegers made good use of the strategic weaknesses of Fort Frontenac, and the seventy-man garrison surrendered before Bradstreet's cannon had spent their twenty-four-hour supply of ammunition.[21]

The attack on Fort Frontenac was a raid into untenable territory, a raid to offset Abercromby's failure at Fort Carillon. Fort Frontenac was not held, it was burned. The French lake fleet was not taken over, it too was burned. Bradstreet's force returned to Albany with talk that the capture of Fort Frontenac

> ... has depriv'd the enemy of Lake Ontario; has frustrated their scheme of making an incursion into this province

[New York]; has kept the Five Nations in a state of neutrality; has influenced the Indians on the frontiers of Pensilvania, Jersey and Virginia to a peace; has facilitated the expedition against fort DuQuesne; has broken the chain of attachment and interest, which subsisted between the French and Indians on the Ohio; and has laid open to us, the easy acquisition and peaceable possession of those immense and valuable tracts, which border on the Ohio, the lakes, and the surrounding country.[22]

Frontenac was really only a fort and, according to Montcalm, ". . . in truth was good for nothing, . . ."[23] Yet Montcalm made sure that he and the French regulars were in no way associated with its loss. In writing to the Minister of War, Montcalm leaves all the blame with Vaudreuil.[24] In the two actions at Fort Carillon and Fort Frontenac, Montcalm won twice, Canada won once and lost once, and Vaudreuil lost twice. For Abercromby, Fort Frontenac helped offset the Fort Carillon fiasco, but was not enough.

Fort Duquesne General John Forbes was assigned the same task in 1758 as Braddock had received in 1755—the capture of Fort Duquesne. Both leaders were tough and determined. Both had trouble raising colonial troops and finding wagons. Both drove a road through the wilderness to Fort Duquesne. There was, however, more contrast than similarity between the two operations. Forbes moved an army of nearly 7,000 men to build a road, while Braddock built a road to move his 5,000-man army. As a road, Forbes' was better planned, better located, better built and better defended. In comparison with Forbes' laborious progress west to Raystown, Pennsylvania, from fortified base to fortified base, Braddock's more circuitous trip was a swift raid. If Braddock had lacked Indian allies because of Governor Dinwiddie (see above, p. 84), Forbes lost almost all of his Indian allies because of the long, slow, uneventful beginning to the campaign of 1758. And yet Forbes' road led, metaphorically, straight to the Treaty of Easton, for the Indians could see a certain winner in this British penetration to Fort Duquesne. While the Fort Duquesne garrison was able to ambush an advance party successfully, the momentum could not be stayed. Braddock's offensive had been destroyed within a few miles of the fort; but, as Forbes' powerful war machine came within a few miles, Fort Duquesne was blown up by its tiny winter garrison.

If fortune favoured the biggest army, it had to favour the Anglo-American offensive of 1758. While the Franco-Canadian forces had seen very little increase and some loss of Indian support, their opponents had increased their forces fourfold since 1755.* Not only this, but the number of British regulars fighting in North America increased fifteen-fold in the same period. The advantages of regular troops were not confined to their willingness to stand in the face of fire, their relative mobility in early spring, or the fact that the size of the conflict was forcing acceptance of a European type of contest upon everyone. The regulars were, in one sense, less vulnerable to guerilla war than were the Americans. Colonial assemblies and militiamen put priority on defence of their people and property, hence their offensive might be abandoned or very severely reduced if guerilla bands of Canadians and Indians were ravaging frontier settlements. But this device would not deter the offensive of British regulars. Perhaps Vaudreuil's offensive was bound to end when it did, and perhaps Pitt's offensive could hardly fail.

The tremendous disparity of forces, and particularly of European forces, was largely due to France's inability to get help across the Atlantic. Admiral Hawke's success of Rochfort in March, 1758,[25] was an indication that it was becoming more difficult to send help. Much of what sounds like callous disregard for Canada in Paris during the winter of 1758-1759, was only realism. Why hand over the few strong ships remaining to France to the mighty British squadrons?

> To send succors in divisions is to run the risk of losing all in detail; to send them together, is to expose ourselves to a general action and to lose all at once....[26]

The British Navy was strangling Canada in 1758. Vaudreuil's offensive had died and the Governor did not have a guerilla-war concept of defence. Though he thought the British would

*The total forces in 1755 approached 11,000, those of 1758 were 44,000.

not attack Quebec in 1759, he always assumed that the city was to be defended in the last extremity.[27] Though Fort Duquesne could be abandoned and destroyed, the forces would not melt into the wilderness, but would retreat to the stand to be made at Quebec. Guerilla war cannot be fought with some specific object to defend—be it a cornfield or a city.

It would have taken an uninformed optimist to see anything less than disaster in store for Canada at the end of 1758. In Paris a war department official wrote:

> . . . we must confine ourselves to treating Canada as a desperate disease is treated, in which the sick man is supported by cordials until he either sink or a crisis save him; . . .[28]

In April, 1759, Montcalm, who was not an optimist, wrote the minister of war:

> Canada will be taken this campaign, and assuredly during the next, if there be not some unforseen good luck, a powerful diversion by sea against the English Colonies, or some gross blunders on the part of the enemy.[29]

The 1758 campaigns could leave him thinking little else. Against odds of nearly three to one in ships, four to one in troops, and ten to one in money,[30] Montcalm was in a pathetic situation. All that could save Canada was peace, and Pitt would give Canada none of that.

1759 — THE CLIMAX?

The drama that unfolded on the Plains of Abraham on September 13, 1759, is inflated in significance if seen in the context of the war. Biographers of General Wolfe are understandably prominent among those who see September 13, 1759, as decisive. Beckles Willson argued:

> Whatever it may have been morally and strategically—and volumes have been written upon it from the military standpoint—politically the battle of Quebec was one of the great battles of the world. By adding Canada to the British Empire it established the supremacy of the Anglo-Saxon race in North America.[31]

How the battle could have added anything to the British Empire without being strategically important is a question worth asking. The most recent defender of Wolfe, after denouncing Brigadier-General George Townshend for losing what Wolfe had won before being wounded, echoes the same note, calling Wolfe:

> ... the youthful commander whose brilliant little masterpiece remains, in its enduring political consequences for the Western world, one of the most notable events in all the annals of war. Without it France might well be ruling yet over the St. Lawrence valley and the territories west of the Alleghenies. . . .[32]

To accept this one must forget a great deal that happened before and after the battle of the Plains of Abraham. Yet even those who do not consider the battle as decisive, or the generalship as brilliant, cannot escape an emphasis on this dramatic, if not romantic, heart of a long struggle. Quebec City, the unattained objective of Phips and Walker, at last fell at the end of a four-day siege following the battle. Taking Quebec might well have been associated with ideas of complete victory and, as has been indicated, the forces gathered for the defence of Quebec City make it clear that the defenders equated the loss of Quebec with defeat. At least the Franco-Canadian forces lost some of their most precious ally—time—in losing Quebec City. In terms of European warfare, and by 1759 this war was being fought largely on European terms, a hostage city was of value at peace negotiations, and winning hostage cities was a good part of winning wars. Taking Quebec was important for what it did to morale on both sides, but it was certainly not a major turning point in this regard. Strategically, Quebec was a beachhead in the core of New France, and a precarious one at that.

Is it just as valid to view the battle as a colourful but clumsy attempt at a *coup de grâce*, rather than as a decisive clash? Alternatively, is the ultimate decision not apparent until after the failure of the Franco-Canadian counterattack in the spring of 1760?

Coup de Grâce? Consider the case for claiming that New France was beaten before September 13, 1759. France had already given up Canada as lost. No help of any consequence was sent to Canada, and a planned invasion of England was little short of insane. If the French navy could not elude the superior British fleet in the spacious Atlantic or the Gulf of St. Lawrence, and if the French government assumed defeat in the event of an encounter—as it did—how could anything be attempted in the British-controlled Channel? Pitt was right in refusing to panic at the rumours of invasion, and before the end of August, 1759, Admiral Boscawen had defeated and destroyed a sizeable squadron of the weaker French fleet in Lagos Bay.

The Indians, too, had almost all given up Canada as lost. Forbes' drive to Fort Duquesne convinced most of the western tribes that it was time to join the baggage train of the British. Those that were not yet convinced learned in the course of the spring and summer of 1759 that it was very difficult to raid successfully along the Forbes road.[33] The lance which had been driven into the western flank of New France was not to be dislodged. The Iroquois, too, had seen the handwriting on the wall. While they were not anxious to see either band of white men win, there was now no question of remaining neutral. The only course was to join with the British, and by early spring of 1759 this course was taken.[34] When Prideaux, succeeded by Sir William Johnson, besieged Fort Niagara and sealed the doom of the West in July of 1759, his force of more than 5,000 men included over 1,000 Indians.

New France was shrivelling rapidly in 1759. Both ends of her St. Lawrence lifeline had been cut. In addition, Fort Carillon and Fort St. Frédéric had been abandoned in the face of Amherst's 8,000-man force, which was slowly but relentlessly doing for this extension of New France what Forbes' methodical invasion had done in the west. The defenders of New France were surrounded and outnumbered in August, 1759, as surely as they were in September of 1760, when they surrendered without a fight at Montreal—with three British armies in attendance. Whether Wolfe's (to be Murray's) army wintered at Quebec or Louisbourg was incidental—New France was already living on borrowed time, time to be measured by the marching feet of the Anglo-American armies. Thus might run the argument that Wolfe could not conquer Canada because it was already beaten.

Beach-head. But New France may not have been beaten until long after the fall of Quebec. If the outcome was substantially affected by Wolfe's victory, was not much of this influence lost in the second battle on the Plains—the Battle of Ste. Foy? Wolfe had forced an army, roughly equal in numbers to his own,[35] to yield the field and thereby Quebec. Disparity in casualties was small,[36] and regardless of the extent of confusion in retreat, the Franco-Canadian army was neither captured, reduced, nor kept from its up-river supply lines.

The battle of Ste. Foy was different. Lévis led a force of nearly 7,000 men, nearly 4,000 of whom were regulars, against Murray's force of some 3,886. Murray's force had been reduced and weakened by scurvy and went into battle at a disadvantage beyond that of their small numbers. Lévis was short of artillery and powder, which suggests that the British might have been advised to stay in the city and defend it from the ramparts. On the other hand, who knew the weaknesses of a fort better than those who, until recently, had been defending it? Murray decided to attack, as Montcalm had done, and the result was a battle bloodier than that of the previous autumn and a victory for Lévis which was more obvious than that of Wolfe. Murray recorded his casualties at 1,104, Lévis his at 833.[37] But in retreat, Murray's army fell back within the city. Lévis' siege was lifted by the arrival of the first British ships, in the second week of May, 1760.

C. P. Stacey suggests:

> This was really the end. British sea power had dealt its final, fatal blow to New France. The rest of the year's operations was merely a leisurely march towards a foregone conclusion.[38]

Lévis had realized that the siege could only succeed with French reinforcements. While he certainly could not be blamed for hoping these would arrive, it might be argued that their failure to arrive was already inevitable. G. S. Graham writes:

> ... the victory on the Plains did not secure Canada or even

Pitt's Offensive, 1758-1760 ❖ 127

clinch Quebec; not until the decisive battle of Quiberon Bay in the following November was the French power of intervention finally extinguished, and the way paved for the reduction of an isolated colony.[39]

Whether New France was doomed by the beginning of 1759, by the battle of Quiberon Bay or by the raising of Lévis' siege in May of 1760, it seems evident that New France's fate was not decided on the Plains of Abraham on September 13, 1759.

* * *

By the time Murray began moving a force of 2,200 men toward Montreal in July, 1760, it was evident that the Canadians considered the war as lost. Desertion was rampant as some Canadians attempted to defend their own homes—only to bring down vengeance upon themselves, though a much more discriminating vengeance than that authorized by Wolfe in the summer of 1759.[40] Many Canadians accepted the inevitable, laying down their arms and taking a British oath of allegiance. This trying reduction of Lévis' tiny army was not confined to the Canadians and the Indians who deserted *en masse*. Lévis records some 548 regular soldiers as deserters and another 122 as absent from their regiments.[41] With little more than 2,000 regular soldiers and less than 1,000 militiamen, all Lévis' skill and protestations about dishonourable surrender could not alter the fact that his situation was pathetic. Amherst, via the upper St. Lawrence, Lieutenant-Colonel William Haviland, via the Richelieu River route, and Murray, from Quebec, succeeded in concentrating some 17,000 troops at Montreal. As Vaudreuil knew, there was no choice but to capitulate. It is somewhat ironic that the tiny French garrison was not allowed the honours of war because of

> a series of bad behaviour in the French during the present war in the country, in setting on the Indians to commit the most shocking cruelties; . . .[42]

European warfare, the acceptance of which made a military solution possible, had triumphed.

Epilogue: Sugar or Snow

Military conquest was not necessarily final victory, as the New England conquerors of Louisbourg realized after that fortress had been exchanged for Madras in 1748. The impressive chain of British victories that empounded France's empire in America, the West Indies, and India by the end of 1762, even the British capture of Havana and the Philippines from France's Spanish ally, did not ensure that Canada would not be returned at the peace table.

In Britain the King and the minister associated with military victory were both missing when peace was finally made. The defence of Hanover had been of vital importance to the second Hanoverian King of Britain. Though he disliked Pitt and Frederick II, George II was so much in favour of an aggressive policy that his peace price in the winter of 1759-1760 was high enough to be considered unrealistic by William Pitt himself. George III, by contrast, was the first British Hanoverian. He was anxious to extricate his country from European entanglements and to give his people peace and himself popularity. Lord Bute, tutor, friend and confidante of the twenty-two-year-old King, was anxious to serve his master, and most prominent ministers concurred for reasons of loyalty, concern over mounting war debts, or fear of fighting the combined forces of France and Spain.

Pitt's last year in office (1761) saw the beginnings of peace negotiations, but progress was hampered by Pitt's unyielding demands, his waning influence in the cabinet, and the strengthening of the French position as an alliance with Spain matured. With a clear view of the failure of the negotiations, and of Spanish entry into the war, Pitt called for a declaration of war on Spain. His colleagues and his King did not agree, though they would declare war on Spain within three months of Pitt's resignation over the issue.

France may have lost the war, but she would win the peace. French Foreign Minister, Étienne François, comte de Stainville, duc de Choiseul, used his court influence, and his diplomatic skills to be the builder of the Peace of Paris. As early as February, 1760, the British were informed of French willingness to cede all of Canada except Île Royale.[1] The British ministry's anxiety about achieving peace made them embarrassed by the string of British victories in 1762, and Choiseul was able to minimize the effect of these upon arrangements. The British abandoned their subsidy policy towards Prussia and were actually making a separate peace with France. (Even if the Anglo-French and Austro-Prussian contests are viewed as separate, both the British and the Prussians knew that the British policy constituted abandonment of an ally.) Choiseul could and did make the most of the situation. Well might Pitt harangue the House of Commons that he approved France's restoration of Minorca to Britain.

> ... and that, he said, was the only conquest which France had to restore; and for this island we have given the East Indies, the West Indies, and Africa. The purchase was made at a price that was fifty times more than it was worth.[2]

Pitt was exaggerating, but Choiseul had won the peace. Canada had paid the peace-table debts of Louis XIV in 1714; in 1763 Canada was a hostage worth sacrificing to regain the more valuable parts of the French empire. Choiseul fought for a fishing base in the St. Lawrence and won. At no time during the protracted negotiations did he fight for the restoration of Canada.

Why did the British negotiators accept a half-continent of snow and bush instead of an island of sugar, or all of the rich French sugar islands? The popular pamphlets of 1761 argued the relative merits of Canada and Guadeloupe.[3] Guadeloupe alone produced more sugar than all of the British West Indies, and the trade and revenue from that island would have helped compensate the victorious British for their war costs. In addition to providing a quick return, Guadeloupe could be more easily supervised with the Royal Navy than could the interior of a continent. Some of those who argued for the retention of Guadeloupe foresaw difficulties between Britain and her American colonies if the French threat was removed from Canada.

Those who argued for retaining Canada pointed out that the war started on the Canadian-American frontier, and if the peace did not settle this issue it would settle nothing. Revival of the French threat would cost Britain and her colonies a fortune in defence. The new lands of the interior were seen as "room enough to settle vast multitudes of industrious people"[4] who would enhance the strength of Britain.

The debate was essentially an academic one, although there was a good deal of self-interest evident. West Indian planters, who were not anxious to see more sugar-producing islands added to the British empire, were in agreement with the majority of Americans in calling for the choice of Canada. It can be argued that the British accepted potential customers rather than real producers of raw materials, and in this can be seen evidence that an empire of markets was replacing an empire of producers. No doubt one of the factors deciding Canada's fate was Choiseul's view of Canada as dispensable in a plan to revive French marine power. The essential parts of the French trading empire, participation in the slave, sugar, and fish trades, had priority.

The Peace of Paris, unlike the Peace of Utrecht, did not usher in a period of Anglo-French *entente*. Though the peace was certainly not harsh, the military victories of the British had humiliated the French, and the peace did not deprive France of the power to seek revenge. Britain had lost the sympathy of Prussia because of the desertion in the last years of the war. The year 1763 saw the beginning of a diplomatic isolation of Britain that would show its full consequences in the American War of Independence. This war became France's war of revenge.

* * *

In reflecting on the struggle for Canada it is possible to distinguish two related, but distinct, contests—the fight over the

Epilogue: Sugar or Snow ❖ 131

kind of weapons and rules, and the duel itself. This essay has argued that, while it did not precede the duel in time or importance, the struggle over weapons and rules was significant. North American pride in the ways of the New World has often led to the assumption that, in warfare as in everything else, the new men of the New World were better than the history-laden men of the Old. The defeat of General Braddock or the later success of the American Revolution can, with some misrepresentation, be seen as evidence of this superiority. Yet, it is obvious that, in the climax of the Anglo-French struggle, the Europeans came and forced their kind of warfare on the wilderness. While guerilla tactics found a place in European strategy, they had lost their own strategic function.

The eclipse of guerilla warfare had a variety of causes. Stouter forts erected between 1714 and 1740 may have made the change inevitable. Well-placed forts could occasionally interfere with the swift, water transport of a raiding party, yet they seldom stopped raids or fell to raiding parties. Larger forces, usually using cannon, meant lines of supply for food, ammunition and the transporting of heavy guns were necessary. Supply lines themselves required defending, and so forts engendered more forts. The European courts had planted seeds of their kind of war when they had built forts in the New World.

In the Anglo-American army there was relatively little struggle over adoption of the essentials of European warfare. Siege warfare had been the essence of New England's warfare since 1689. To utilize American strength, with a minimum of training for most recruits, European conventional warfare had clear advantages. As long as the Americans fought like guerillas, they were wasting their major advantage—manpower. The large influx of British troops after 1755, as well as more direct control of the fighting from Britain, ensured complete acceptance of conventional warfare. Colonial rangers were well-paid, well-respected, and in high demand, but most of their work was to provide a protective screen for the regular army, a task as incompatible with guerilla warfare as defending a city.[5] Though Indian alliances were important, Indian allies were not. For the Anglo-American forces, the climax to the long struggle with Canada was a white man's war.

The Franco-Canadian situation was vastly different. Indian warriors and Canadian *coureurs de bois* were numerous and effective enough to match American guerillas. Canadian-born Governor Vaudreuil was committed to full use of guerillas, even when he knew that his opponents would attack in 1758. He could see the defence of Canada in harrying communication lines, attacking outposts and winning time, as he and many of his predecessors had done. Montcalm insisted on a tighter, conventional defence of Canada, and his success at Fort Carillon was enough to confirm the French court's prejudice in the same direction. Three weeks after the defence of Fort Carillon one of Montcalm's aides had proclaimed:

> Now war is established here on the European basis. Projects for the campaign, for armies, for artillery, for seiges, for battles. It no longer is a matter of making a raid, but of conquering or being conquered. What a revolution! What a change![6]

It is very unlikely that Vaudreuil's policy could have saved Canada or even have postponed its fall. He could not see, or would not see, that the Anglo-American offensive was aimed at capturing Quebec City, a European citadel in the physical and psychological sense. Nor did he fully appreciate that this war was different from its predecessors, in that winning time was no solution. The British were committed to victory in North America. Given the odds, there was very little chance anything could save Canada. By 1758 the Europeans, French and British alike, had completed the imposition of their kind of fighting upon the struggle in North America. By doing so they increased the odds, which were already overwhelmingly in favour of those who were soon to win.

The fall of Canada may have had important cultural consequences, but it did not have cultural causes. Canada did not fall because of absolutism, paternalism, Catholicism or the seigneurial régime. Canada was not defeated primarily because of cheaper British trade goods, limited grain supply, a narrowly based economy, or the numerical preponderance of the American colonies. The British Army and the Royal Navy besieged Canada with an overwhelming military force. France could not send a force to lift the siege and, after a stout defence, Canada fell to fortune's favourite—the biggest army. Is this not sufficient reason for the fall of Canada?

Notes

ABBREVIATIONS

AHR—*American Historical Review*
CHA Booklet—The Canadian Historical Association Booklets
CHA Report—*Canadian Historical Association Report*
CHR—*Canadian Historical Review*
C.S.P.C.—*Calendar of State Papers, Colonial Series*
EHR—*English Historical Review*
MVHR—*Mississippi Valley Historical Review*
NEQ—*New England Quarterly*
N.Y.C.D.—*Documents Relative to the Colonial History of the State of New York*
R.A.P.Q.—*Rapport de l'Archiviste de la Province de Québec*
W&MQ—*William and Mary Quarterly*

Introduction

1. Michel Brunet, "The British Conquest: Canadian Social Scientists and the Fate of the Canadiens," *CHR*, vol. XL (1959), pp. 106/7.
2. Cotton Mather, *Decennium Luctuosum*, reprinted in C. H. Lincoln, *Narratives of the Indian Wars* (New York, 1913), p. 206.
3. Guy Frégault's biographies, *Iberville le Conquérant* (Montreal, 1944) and *Le Grand Marquis: Pierre de Rigaud de Vaudreuil, et la Louisiane* (Montreal, 1952) make evident the merits of leading Canadians, while his *François Bigot, Administrateur français,* 2 vols. (Montreal, 1948) would have this peculating nabob's approach to Canada seen as representative of French administrators in Canada. In *La Guerre de la Conquête* (Montreal, 1955) Frégault presents a critique of Montcalm which serves as an antidote to some traditional hero-worship.
4. Gustave Lanctôt, *A History of Canada,* 3 vols. (Toronto, 1963-65), vol. III, p. 197.
5. Francis Parkman, *Montcalm and Wolfe,* 12th ed., 2 vols. (Boston, 1888), vol. I, p. 35.
6. Howard H. Peckham, *The Colonial Wars 1689-1762* (Chicago, 1964), pp. 216/17.
7. See H. G. Peterson, "The Military Equipment of the Plymouth and Bay Colonies, 1670-1690," *NEQ,* vol. XX (1947), pp. 197-208.

NOTES FOR PAGES 6 TO 25

8. Quoted in D. J. Boorstin, *The Americans: The Colonial Experience* (New York, 1958), p. 346.

Chapter I

1. *Private Correspondence of Sarah, Duchess of Marlborough*, 2nd ed. (London, 1838), vol. II, p. 419.
2. Nellis M. Crouse, *The French Struggle for the West Indies, 1665-1713* (New York, 1943), p. 215.
3. G. S. Graham, *Empire of the North Atlantic*, 2nd ed. (Toronto, 1958), ch. iv.
4. Guy Frégault, "L'Empire britannique et la conquête du Canada, 1700-1713," *Revue d'Histoire de l'Amerique française*, vol. X (1956), pp. 154/55; Franklin B. Dexter, "Estimates of Population in the American Colonies," *American Antiquarian Society Proceedings*, new series, vol. V (1888), p. 22.
5. Howard H. Peckham, *The Colonial Wars 1689-1762* (Chicago, 1964), pp. 216/17.
6. See W. J. Eccles, *The Government of New France*, CHA Booklet No. 18 (Ottawa, 1965) and Chapter III of his *Canada under Louis XIV, 1663-1701* (Toronto, 1964).
7. Marcel Trudel, *The Seigneurial Régime*, CHA Booklet No. 6 (Ottawa, 1956) and E. R. Adair, "The French-Canadian Seigneury," *CHR*, vol. XXXV (1954), pp. 187-207.
8. See Cameron Nish, "The Nature, Composition, and Functions of the Canadian Bourgeoisie," *CHA Annual Report for 1966* (Ottawa, 1967), pp. 14-28, for a thoughtful discussion of the work done on this topic.
9. Eccles, *Canada under Louis XIV*, p. 99.
10. *Ibid.*, p. 204.
11. Intendant Jean Rochart de Champigny, "Mémoire instructif sur le Canada," *Bulletin des Recherches Historiques*, vol. XXII (1916), pp. 278/79.
12. G. F. G. Stanley, *Canada's Soldiers, 1604-1954* (Toronto, 1954), pp. 25-28.
13. Eccles, *Canada under Louis XIV*, pp. 150-52.
14. G. T. Hunt, *The Wars of the Iroquois* (Madison, 1940), ch. xi.
15. Eccles, *Canada under Louis XIV*, pp. 174/75.
16. See Hunt, *op. cit.*, p. 154, for statistics on population.
17. Anonymous, *An Essay upon the Government of the English Plantations on the Continent of America* (London, 1701), preface.
18. Quoted in Viola F. Barnes, *The Dominion of New England* (New Haven, 1923), p. 53n.
19. *N.Y.C.D.*, vol. III, p. 581.
20. *C.S.P.C. 1689-92* (No. 513), p. 167.
21. Quoted from "Frontiers Well-Defended," in Barnes, *op. cit.*, p. 214n. Also see Daniel Neal, *The History of New England* ..., 2 vols. (London, 1720), vol. II, pp. 456/57.
22. Cotton Mather, *Decennium Luctuosum*, reprinted in C. H. Lincoln, *Narratives of the Indian Wars* (New York, 1913), p. 242.

NOTES FOR PAGES 25 TO 34

23. *A Narrative of the Proceedings of Sir Edmond Androsse* . . . , quoted in Michael G. Hall, *et alia, The Glorious Revolution in America* (Chapel Hill, 1964), p. 35.
24. Thomas Church, *The History of the Great Indian War of 1675 and 1676* . . . (Boston, 1825), pp. 192/93.
25. *Ibid.*, p. 210. Church would attack Acadia in 1696 and 1704, terrorizing defenceless settlements in the Bay of Fundy, but not assaulting the fort at Port Royal, as Phips did in 1690, and Colonel John March did twice in 1707.
26. Barnes, *op. cit.*, pp. 218/19.
27. See J. T. Adams, *Revolutionary New England, 1691-1775* (Boston, 1923), pp. 64/5.
28. Mark van Doren's preface to *The Life of Sir William Phips*, a eulogy by Cotton Mather (New York, 1929), p. ix.
29. Mather, *Decennium Luctuosum*, p. 214.
30. The flagship, *Six Friends*, carried 44 guns. Mather, *Phips*, pp. 68/9.
31. Duncan Grinnell-Milne, in defending Wolfe's delays, points out that the prevailing westerlies are usually replaced by seasonal easterlies late in September. *Mad, Is He? The Character and Achievements of James Wolfe* (London, 1963), p. 13.
32. Major Walley's Journal, reprinted in Ernest Myrand, *Sir William Phips devant Québec* (Quebec, 1893), p. 38.
33. Relation du Major Thomas Savage, in Myrand, *ibid.*, p. 50.
34. Neal, *op. cit.*, vol. II, p. 464.
35. J. T. Adams, *The Founding of New England* (Boston, 1921), p. 441.
36. Major Walley's Journal, in Myrand, *op. cit.*, pp. 46/7.
37. Francis Parkman, *Count Frontenac and New France under Louis XIV*, 19th ed. (Boston, 1888), p. 277.
38. In 1689, Albany paid two to four times as much for furs as did the Canadian merchants. See A. H. Buffinton, "The Policy of Albany and English Westward Expansion," *MVHR*, vol. VIII (1921-22), p. 337.
39. C. M. Andrews, *The Colonial Period of American History*, 4 vols. (New Haven, 1934-38), vol. III, p. 102.
40. A. W. Trelease, *Indian Affairs in Colonial New York: The Seventeenth Century* (Ithaca, N.Y., 1960), p. 213.
41. *N.Y.C.D.*, vol. III, p. 575.
42. See A. W. Trelease, "The Iroquois and the Western Fur Trade: A Problem in Interpretation," *MVHR*, vol. XLIX (1962-63), pp. 32-51.
43. J. Lunn, "The Illegal Fur Trade Out of New France, 1713-60," *CHA Report for 1939*, p. 65.
44. A. H. Buffinton, "The Colonial Wars and Their Results," in A. C. Flick, ed., *History of the State of New York*, 10 vols. (Albany, 1933-37), vol. II, p. 217.
45. Trelease, *op. cit*, p 216; *N.Y.C.D.*, vol. IV, pp. 337/38. The Iroquois were estimated to have lost more than half of their warriors in this war too. *Ibid.*
46. *N.Y.C.D.*, vol. III, pp. 390, 394.

NOTES FOR PAGES 34 TO 64

47. Richard S. Dunn, *Puritans and Yankees* (Princeton, 1962), pp. 177/79, 195/98, 208.

Chapter II

1. To Robert Hunter, February 6, 1710/11, printed in Gerald S. Graham, *The Walker Expedition to Quebec, 1711* (Toronto, 1953), pp. 276/77.
2. See, for example, Board of Trade report to the King, March 2, 1715/16, *C.S.P.C. 1716-17*, No. 70.
3. Quoted in Yves F. Zoltvany, "The Problem of Western Policy under Philippe de Rigaud de Vaudreuil, 1703-1725," *CHA Report for 1964*, p. 16.
4. *Ibid.*, pp. 16/7.
5. These tentative figures are drawn from Howard H. Peckham, *The Colonial Wars 1689-1762* (Chicago, 1964), pp. 53, 74/5.
6. This policy is discussed by G. M. Waller, "New York's Role in Queen Anne's War, 1702-1713," *New York History*, vol. XXXIII (1952), pp. 40-53.
7. Quoted in A. M. Wilson, *French Foreign Policy during the Administration of Cardinal Fleury, 1726-1743* (Cambridge, Mass., 1936), p. 65.
8. See, for example, W. Keith to the Board of Trade, Feb. 16, 1719, *C.S.P.C., 1719-20*, No. 61i; Board of Trade to the King, Sept. 8, 1721, *C.S.P.C., 1720-21*, No. 656; Vaudreuil and Bégon to the minister, Sept. 20, 1714, *R.A.P.Q., 1947-8*, pp. 272-288; Vaudreuil to duc d'Orleans, Feb., 1716, *ibid.*, pp. 291/95.
9. Francis Parkman, *A Half-Century of Conflict*, 2 vols. (Boston, 1892), vol. II, p. 73.
10. *Ibid.*, p. 135.
11. S. E. Morison, *The Oxford History of the American People* (New York, 1965), p. 156.
12. G. M. Wrong, ed., "Lettre d'un Habitant de Louisbourg," *University of Toronto Studies in History and Economics*, vol. I (1897), p. 15. For the defensive posture of Massachusetts in 1744 see J. S. McLennan, *Louisbourg from Its Foundation to Its Fall* (London, 1918), p. 128.
13. John A. Schutz, *William Shirley, King's Governor of Massachusetts* (Chapel Hill, 1961), ch. v.
14. Robert E. Wall, "Louisbourg, 1745," *NEQ*, vol. XXXVII (1964), pp. 64-83.
15. Schutz, *op. cit.*, p. 96. G. S. Graham, *Empire of the North Atlantic*, 2nd ed. (Toronto, 1958), p. 128.
16. "Lettre d'un Habitant de Louisbourg," pp. 37/8.
17. Parkman, *op. cit.*, vol. II, p. 172.
18. *The Correspondence of William Shirley*, ed. C. H. Lincoln, 2 vols. (New York, 1912), vol. II, p. 13. For a similar position on the part of the French ministry, see *N.Y.C.D.*, vol. X, p. 270.
19. Lawrence Henry Gipson, *The British Empire before the American Revolution*, 14 vols. (Caldwell, Idaho and New York, 1936-1969), vol. IV, pp. 265/66.
20. *Ibid.*, p. 298.

Chapter III

1. Guy Frégault, "Le Régime Seigneurial et l'Expansion de la

NOTES FOR PAGES 64 TO 73

Colonisation dans le Bassin du Saint-Laurent au dix-huitième Siècle," *CHA Report for 1944* (Ottawa, 1945), pp. 61-73.
2. *Peter Kalm's Travels,* ed. A. B. Benson (New York, 1937), vol. II, pp. 588/89.
3. *Military Affairs in North America, 1748-1765,* ed. Stanley Pargellis (New York, 1936), pp. xiv-xv.
4. *Ibid.,* p. 66; G. de T. Glazebrook, "Roads in New France and the Policy of Expansion," *CHA Report for 1934* (Ottawa, 1935), pp. 51/2.
5. Lawrence Henry Gipson, *The British Empire Before the American Revolution,* 14 vols. (Caldwell, Idaho and New York, 1936-1969), vol. VII, p. 200.
6. *Ibid.,* vol. IV, pp. 101, 106/7.
7. Verner W. Crane, *The Southern Frontier, 1670-1732* (Durham, N.C., 1928), pp. 59, 63, 208, 221, 222, 230.
8. *The Correspondence of William Shirley,* vol. II, pp. 133/34.
9. *N.Y.C.D.,* vol. X, p. 222.
10. See *The French Régime,* ed. Cameron Nish (Scarborough, Ont., 1965), pp. 145/46.
11. Guy Frégault, "La guerre de Sept ans et la civilisation canadienne," *Revue d'histoire de l'Amérique française,* vol. VII (1953-4), pp. 202/3.
12. Gipson, *op. cit.,* vol. V, pp. 39-41.
13. *N.Y.C.D.,* vol. X, p. 244.
14. *Ibid.,* p. 223.
15. Pargellis, *op. cit.,* p. 163.
16. Gustave Lanctôt, *A History of Canada,* 3 vols. (Toronto, 1963-65), vol. III, ch. xii; Gipson, *op. cit.,* vol. V, pp. 23/6.
17. Lanctôt, *op. cit.,* vol. III, p. 118.
18. E. R. Adair, "Anglo-French Rivalry in the Fur Trade during the Eighteenth Century," *Culture,* vol. VIII (1947), p. 447.
19. Jean Lunn, "Agriculture and War in Canada, 1740-1760," *CHR,* vol. XVI (1935), pp. 123-136; for grain shortage in 1755 see Frégault, *François Bigot, Administrateur français,* 2 vols. (Montreal, 1948), vol. II, p. 112.
20. Gipson, *op. cit.,* vol. IV, p. 139/40.
21. Lunn, *loc. cit.,* pp. 133/36.
22. Frégault, *François Bigot, op. cit,* vol. II, pp. 122, 126.
23. Frégault, "La guerre de Sept ans et la Civilisation canadienne," p. 188.
24. Gipson, *op. cit.,* vol. V, pp. 26/7.
25. Lanctôt, *op. cit.,* vol. III, p. 121.
26. Frégault, *François Bigot,* vol. II, pp. 127/29.
27. Gipson, *op. cit.,* vol. V, pp. 27/8.
28. Compare the statistics in Carl Bridenbaugh's *Cities in the Wilderness,* p. 6n with those in his *Cities in Revolt* (New York, 1955), p. 216.
29. E. B. Greene, *Provincial America* (New York, 1905), p. 245.
30. Bridenbaugh, *Cities in the Wilderness,* pp. 96/7; Frank Thistlethwaite, "The Development of the American Communities, 2. North America," *New Cambridge Modern History,* vol. VII, *The Old Regime, 1713-63* (Cambridge, 1963), p. 509.
31. J. Mitchell, *The Contest in America between Great Britain and France* (London, 1757), pp. 137/38.
32. Quoted in Gipson, *op. cit.,* vol. V, pp. 134/35.

33. *Ibid.,* p. 163.
34. *Pennsylvania Archives,* 4th series, vol. II, p. 373.
35. *Parliamentary History,* vol. XV, p. 771.
36. Horace Walpole, May 14, 1754. Quoted in L. H. Gipson, "A French Project for Victory Short of a Declaration of War, 1755," *CHR,* vol. XXVI (1945), p. 362.
37. This evolution of policy is well described in Stanley M. Pargellis, *Lord Loudoun in North America* (New Haven, 1933), pp. 22-34.
38. Thomas Potter's speech of Nov. 14, 1754. *Parliamentary History,* vol. XV, p. 342.
39. William Beckford, *ibid.,* p. 355.
40. A. T. Mahan, *The Influence of Sea Power Upon History, 1660-1783* (Boston, 1890), p. 291.
41. Quoted in Gipson, *op. cit.,* vol. VI, p. 109.
42. See G. S. Graham, *Empire of the North Atlantic,* 2nd ed. (Toronto, 1958), p. 159; Gipson, *op. cit.,* vol. VI, p. 118.
43. *N.Y.C.D.,* vol. X, pp. 265, 270.
44. Frégault, "La guerre de Sept ans et la civilisation canadienne," pp. 186, 194. The 'punch line' of a set of private instructions issued to Governor Vaudreuil in April of 1756 asked him to be cautious and to reconcile all activities "... with the views of the greatest economy, which he must make his principle study in every sort of expense." *N.Y.C.D.,* vol. X, p. 294.
45. R. Pares, "American Versus Continental Warfare, 1739-1763," *EHR,* vol. LI (1936), p. 451. Pares goes on to point out that in 1760 the French navy received about one-seventh the allotment given the British navy for ordinary expenses. The French army would also be seriously hampered by financial limitations. Walter L. Dorn, *Competition for Empire, 1740-1763* (New York, 1940), p. 85.
46. Quoted in Frégault, *La Guerre de la Conquête* (Montréal, 1955), p. 317.

Chapter IV

1. *Military Affairs in North America, 1748-1765,* ed. Stanley Pargellis (New York, 1936), p. 83.
2. Lawrence Henry Gipson, *The British Empire before the American Revolution,* 14 vols. (Caldwell, Idaho and New York, 1936-1969), vol. VI, pp. 64/5, 77.
3. *Travels in New France by J.C.B.,* Sylvester Stevens, *et alia,* eds. (Harrisburg, 1941), p. 74.
4. Guy Frégault, *La Guerre de la Conquête* (Montreal, 1955), p. 138; Gipson, *op. cit.,* vol. VI, p. 91.
5. Frégault, *op. cit.,* p. 140.
6. Braddock's expedition is carefully studied in Gipson, *op. cit.,* vol. VI, ch. iv, and in Stanley M. Pargellis, "Braddock's Defeat," *AHR,* vol. XLI (1936), pp. 253/69.
7. Quoted in Gipson, *op. cit.,* vol. VI, p. 151.
8. J. R. Cuneo, *Robert Rogers of the Rangers* (New York, 1959), pp. 21 ff.
9. *N.Y.C.D.,* vol. X, p. 317.
10. *Report of the Canadian Archives for 1905,* vol. II, Appendix C, p. 56.
11. See Eric Robson, "The Armed Forces and the Art of War,"

NOTES FOR PAGES 93 TO 107

New Cambridge Modern History, vol. VII, p. 174.
12. J. B. Brebner, "Canadian Policy Towards the Acadians in 1751," *CHR* (1931), pp. 284-86. Brebner's *New England's Outpost: Acadia before the Conquest of Canada* (New York, 1927), is still perhaps the best general study of the topic.
13. Stanley M. Pargellis, *Lord Loudoun in North America* (New Haven, 1933), p. 37.
14. *Ibid.*
15. *Ibid.,* p. 41.
16. Pargellis, *Military Affairs in North America,* p. 136.
17. Pargellis, *Lord Louden,* chapter 2.
18. Pargellis, *Military Affairs,* p. 141.

Chapter V

1. See, for instance, Vaudreuil's account of affairs to August 20, 1756, in *N.Y.C.D.,* vol. X, pp. 471/74.
2. *Ibid.,* pp. 423/24.
3. *Ibid.,* p. 484.
4. Hayes Baker-Crothers, *Virginia and the French and Indian War* (Chicago, 1928), ch. v.
5. R. L. D. Davidson, *War Comes to Quaker Pennsylvania, 1682-1756* (New York, 1957), chs. vi-x.
6. *N.Y.C.D.,* vol. X, pp. 391/92.
7. *Ibid.,* pp. 396/97, 400, 481.
8. *Ibid.,* pp. 458, 467, 471.
9. Stanley M. Pargellis, *Lord Loudoun in North America* (New Haven, 1933), pp. 148-162.
10. *N.Y.C.D.,* vol. X, p. 441.
11. *Ibid.,* pp. 440/44, 457-461.
12. *Ibid.,* p. 462.
13. *Ibid.*
14. *Ibid.,* pp. 480, 488/89, 490/92, 497.
15. *Ibid.,* pp. 490/93, 538.
16. *Ibid.,* p. 499.
17. *Ibid.,* pp. 523/26.
18. Guy Frégault, *La Guerre de la Conquête* (Montreal, 1955), pp. 214/15.
19. Vaudreuil was aware of this. *N.Y.C.D.,* vol. X, p. 542.
20. For an account of the mauling of Robert Rogers' company of Rangers by a scouting party, see J. R. Cuneo, *Robert Rogers of the Rangers* (New York, 1959), ch. iv.
21. *N.Y.C.D.,* vol. X, p. 542.
22. *Ibid.,* p. 543.
23. *Ibid.,* p. 551.
24. *Ibid.,* pp. 547/55.
25. *Ibid.,* p. 549.
26. Francis Parkman, *Montcalm and Wolfe,* 12th ed., 2 vols. (Boston, 1888), vol. I, pp. 447-451. See also Howard H. Peckham, *The Colonial Wars 1689-1762* (Chicago, 1964), p. 162.
27. Gustave Lanctôt, *A History of Canada,* 3 vols. (Toronto, 1963-65), vol. III, pp. 145/46.
28. Frégault, *op. cit.,* p. 214.
29. *N.Y.C.D.,* vol. X, pp. 552, 565, 567.
30. *Ibid.,* p. 597.
31. *Ibid.,* p. 567. 'Breed' has been used in place of the translation, or rather lack of translation, of the word "race" in this document.
32. *Ibid.,* p. 574.
33. *Ibid.,* p. 591.
34. *Ibid.,* pp. 591/93.
35. Pargellis, *op. cit.,* pp. 243/44. General Webb's account of the losses under his command was different from Montcalm's.

141

NOTES FOR PAGES 107 TO 125

Webb reported 250 captured and twenty-four boats lost.
36. *N.Y.C.D.,* vol. X, pp. 606-608.
37. Pargellis, *op. cit.,* pp. 224/50.
38. *N.Y.C.D.,* vol. X, p. 597.
39. Pargellis, *op. cit.,* p. 243.
40. *N.Y.C.D.,* vol. X, p. 597.
41. *Knox's Historical Journal of the Campaigns in North America,* ed. A. G. Doughty, 3 vols. (London, 1914-16), vol. I, pp. 181/82.
42. *N.Y.C.D.,* vol. X, pp. 659/66.
43. *Ibid.,* pp. 672/74.
44. *Ibid.,* p. 673.
45. *Ibid.,* p. 658.
46. *Ibid.,* p. 874.
47. *Ibid.,* p. 868.
48. Guy Frégault, *François Bigot, Administrateur français,* 2 vols. (Montreal, 1948), vol. II, pp. 253/57.

Chapter VI

1. Horace Walpole, quoted in Lawrence Henry Gipson, *The British Empire before the American Revolution,* 14 vols. (Caldwell, Idaho and New York, 1936-1969), vol. VII, p. 12.
2. See Rex Whitworth, *Field Marshal Lord Ligonier* (Oxford, 1958), pp. 201-202, 396/97; Eric McDermott, S.J., "The Elder Pitt and His Admirals and Generals," *Military Affairs,* vol. XX (1956), pp. 65-71; and Stanley M. Pargellis, *Lord Loudoun in North America* (New Haven, 1933), ch. xii, which is a critique of Pitt's strategy.
3. Pargellis, *op. cit.,* pp. 358/59.
4. *Ibid.,* p. 358.
5. Gipson, *op. cit.,* vol. VII, p. 43.
6. Pargellis, *op. cit.,* chs. iii and iv.
7. *Ibid.,* pp. 351/55.
8. Gipson, *op. cit.,* vol. VII, p. 103.
9. *Ibid.,* p. 105.
10. J. Mackay Hitsman and C. C. J. Bond, "The Assault Landing at Louisbourg, 1758," *CHR,* vol. XXXV (1954), pp. 323/24.
11. *Ibid.,* pp. 321/22.
12. Gipson, *op. cit.,* vol. VII, p. 195.
13. J. W. Fortescue, *A History of the British Army,* 13 vols. (London, 1899-1930), vol. II, p. 405.
14. Maurice Sautai, *Montcalm at the Battle of Carillon* (Ticonderoga, 19–), pp. 44-51; *N.Y.C.D.,* vol X, pp. 757/61.
15. *N.Y.C.D.,* vol. X, p. 720.
16. Guy Frégault, *La Guerre de la Conquête* (Montreal, 1955), p. 307.
17. Charles Lee, quoted in Gipson, *op. cit.,* vol. VII, p. 227.
18. Fortescue, *op. cit.,* vol. II, p. 328.
19. Frégault, *op. cit.,* p. 305.
20. *An Impartial Account of Lieut. Col. Bradstreet's Expedition to Fort Frontenac* (printed Toronto, 1940), p. 27. Also see Gipson, *op. cit.,* vol. VII, pp. 236/46.
21. *Ibid.,* p. 28.
22. *Ibid.,* p. 30.
23. *N.Y.C.D.,* vol. X, p. 831.
24. *Ibid.*
25. G. S. Graham, *Empire of the North Atlantic,* 2nd ed. (Toronto, 1952), pp. 170/71.
26. *N.Y.C.D.,* vol. X, p. 934.
27. *Ibid.,* pp. 952/58.
28. *Ibid.,* p. 926.
29. *Ibid.,* p. 960.
30. Frégault, *op. cit.,* p. 283.
31. Beckles Willson, *The Life and Letters of James Wolfe* (London, 1909), p. 497.
32. Duncan Grinnell-Milne, *Mad, Is He? The Character and Achievements of James Wolfe*

(London, 1963), p. 288. For the denunciation of Townshend, see pp. 260/65, 270.
33. Gipson, *op. cit.,* vol. VII, pp. 335, 338/39.
34. *Ibid.,* pp. 342/43.
35. See C. P. Stacey, *Quebec 1759: The Siege and the Battle* (Toronto, 1959), p. 141, for a careful treatment of this question.
36. *Ibid.,* p. 152.
37. *Ibid.,* p. 164.
38. *Ibid.,* p. 165.
39. Graham, *op. cit.,* p. 175. See also Gipson, *op. cit.,* vol. VII, p. 437, and Julian S. Corbett, *England in the Seven Years War,* 2 vols. (London, 1907), vol. II, p. 112.
40. Stacey, *op. cit.,* ch. v.
41. *Journal des Campagnes du Chevalier de Lévis en Canada de 1756 à 1760* (Montreal, 1889), p. 315.
42. *Journal of William Amherst in America, 1758-1760,* J. C. Webster, ed. (Toronto, 1931), p. 68.

Epilogue
1. Marjorie G. Reid, "Pitt's Decision to Keep Canada in 1761," *CHA Report for 1926* (Ottawa, 1927), p. 21.
2. *Parliamentary History,* vol. XV, p. 1266.
3. See W. L. Grant, "Canada Versus Guadeloupe, an Episode of the Seven Years' War," *AHR,* vol. XVII (1911-12), pp. 735/43.
4. John Rutherford, *The Importance of the Colonies to Great Britain* (London, 1761), p. 9. See also A. H. Smyth, ed., *The Writings of Benjamin Franklin,* 10 vols. (New York, 1905-07), vol. IV, p. 4.
5. See, for example, John R. Cuneo, *Robert Rogers of the Rangers* (New York, 1959), ch. iv.
6. E. P. Hamilton, ed., *Adventure in the Wilderness: The American Journals of Louis Antoine de Bougainville, 1756-1760* (Norman, Oklahoma, 1964), p. 252.

Bibliographical Note

What follows is only a minute sampling of the vast literature on nearly a century of the history of Europe and North America. Only those works which are particularly relevant for this essay, and relatively available (paperbacks are marked *), are included.

Students interested in exploring particular problems might begin by looking at: J. S. Bromley & A. Goodwin (eds.), *A Select List of Works on Europe and Europe Overseas, 1715-1815,* (Oxford: Oxford University Press, 1956); G. Howe, *et al* (eds.), *Guide to Historical Literature,* (Washington: Macmillan, 1961); O. Handlin, *et al* (eds.), *Harvard Guide to American History,* (Cambridge, Mass.: Atheneum, 1963)*; G. Lanctôt (ed.), *L'Oeuvre de la France en Amérique du Nord: Bibliographie sélective et critique,* (Montreal: Fides, 1951); or Jean Hamelin (ed.), *Guide de l'étudiant en histoire du Canada,* (Quebec: Laval University Press, 1965).

Most of the best collections of printed documents relating to the four wars for America, many of which are cited in the *Notes* above, are long out of print. Recent collections which do print relevant material include: K. A. MacKirdy, *et al., Changing Perspectives in Canadian History* (Toronto: Dent, 1967)*; Cameron Nish, *The French Régime* (Scarborough, Ont.: Prentice-Hall, 1965)*; Michael G. Hall, *et al., The Glorious Revolution in America: Documents on the Colonial Crisis of 1689* (Chapel Hill, N.C.: University of North Carolina Press, 1964)*; and Max Savelle's *The Colonial Origins of American Thought* (New York: Van Nostrand, 1964)*. Two particularly relevant contemporary pamphlets have recently been reprinted: *State of the British and French Colonies in North America* (London, 1755 [reprinted, New York, Johnson Reprint, 1967]) and John Mitchell's *The Contest in America between Great Britain and France with Its Consequences and Importance* (London, 1757 [reprinted, New York: Johnson Reprint, 1965]).

The most comprehensive and detailed narrative of the Anglo-French struggle for North America is still the classic work of Francis

Parkman, *France and England in North America*, 9 vols. (Boston: Little, Brown, 1865-92), several volumes of which are in paperback: *The Conspiracy of Pontiac* (New York: Collier)*; *Count Frontenac and New France under Louis XIV* (Boston: Beacon)*; *Discovery of the Great West: La Salle* (New York: Holt, Rinehart and Winston)*; *A Half Century of Conflict* (New York: Collier)*; *Montcalm and Wolfe* (New York: Collier)*. Parkman's presuppositions have been challenged directly by W. J. Eccles, "History of New France According to Francis Parkman," *W&MQ*, 3rd series, XVIII (1961), pp. 163-75. Parkman's use of evidence has been scrutinized by R. C. Vitzthum, "The Historian as Editor: Francis Parkman's Reconstruction of Sources in Montcalm and Wolfe," *Journal of American History*, LIII (1966-7), pp. 471-86. Howard H. Peckham's *The Colonial Wars, 1689-1762* (Chicago: University of Chicago Press, 1964)* is a compact and readable military narrative which frequently reveals the enduring appeal of some of Parkman's assumptions.

The colonial wars are put in the context of European imperial struggles in Edmond Préclin, *Le XVIIIe Siècle*. 2 vols. (Paris: Presses universitaires de France, 1952)*, Pierre Muret, *La Prépondérance Anglaise, 1715-1763* (Paris: Presses universitaires de France, 1949)*, or in the three relevant volumes of W. L. Langer (ed.), *The Rise of Modern Europe*: J. B. Wolf, *The Emergence of the Great Powers, 1685-1715* (New York: Harper, 1951)*; Penfield Roberts, *The Quest for Security, 1715-1740* (New York: Harper, 1947)*; and particularly W. L. Dorn, *Competition for Empire, 1740-1763* (New York: Harper, 1940)*. These five works all have very useful bibliographies; the otherwise helpful *New Cambridge Modern History*, Vol. VII, J. O. Lindsay (ed.), *The Old Regime 1713-1763* (Cambridge: Cambridge University Press, 1963), does not. The naval phase of this contest is surveyed in A. T. Mahan *The Influence of Sea Power upon History, 1660-1783* (Boston: Little, Brown, 1889 [reprinted, London: Methuen, 1965])* and is very well treated by G. S. Graham, *Empire of the North Atlantic*. 2nd ed. (Toronto: Oxford, 1958). One of the best histories of the French navy is J. Tramond, *Manuel d'histoire maritime de la France des origines à 1815*, 2nd ed. (Paris: Société d'éditions géographiques, maritimes et coloniales, 1947). Though not covering the whole of the period of struggle, L. H. Gipson's first eight volumes of the fourteen volume

The British Empire before the American Revolution (Caldwell, Idaho: Caxton and New York: Knopf, 1936-69) constitute an incredibly thorough study of the global contest between France and England.

Much of American colonial history forms an integral part of the Anglo-French struggle for North America, and this field of study is rich in available literature. One of the best recent surveys of the field is Clarence Ver Steeg's *The Formative Years, 1607-1763* (New York: Hill & Wang, 1964)* which includes a good introductory bibliography, as does D. J. Boorstin's provocative interpretation *The Americans: The Colonial Experience* (New York: Random House, 1958)*. Another, more selective guide to newer literature is the second edition of L. B. Wright's *New Interpretations of American Colonial History* (New York: Macmillan, 1963)*. In addition to the works of Parkman and Peckham, the American perspective of the "colonial wars" can be seen in the classics of H. L. Osgood, *The American Colonies in the Seventeenth Century*, 3 vols. (New York: Columbia, 1904-7 [reprinted, Gloucester, Mass.: Smith, 1957]) and *The American Colonies in the Eighteenth Century*, 4 vols. (New York: Columbia, 1924-5 [reprinted, Gloucester, Mass.: Smith, 1958]). A recent general study, *The Northern Colonial Frontier, 1607-1763* (New York: Holt, Rinehart and Winston, 1966) by Douglas E. Leach, emphasizes aspects of particular interest in the context of this essay.

In Canadian history, the last seventy years of New France is largely the history of the wars for survival and their relationship to Canadian life. A useful guide to work done on New France is J. C. Rule's, "The Old Regime in America: A Review of Recent Interpretations of France in America," *W&MQ*, 3rd series, XIX (1962), pp. 575-600. G. M. Wrong's *Rise and Fall of New France*, 2 vols. (London: Macmillan, 1928) is still valuable and Gustave Lanctôt's *A History of Canada*, 3 vols. (Toronto: Clarke, Irwin, 1963-65) is a sound statement of a traditional approach. The theme of *la survivance* found its most empassioned statement in the works of Abbé Lionel Groulx, including *Nôtre Grande Aventure: L'Empire français en Amérique du Nord, 1535-1760* (Montreal: Fides, 1958) and *Histoire du Canada français depuis la découverte*, 4 vols. (Montreal: Fides, 1950-52). Guy Frégault has written important works which span the four wars for America, particularly *Iberville le Conquérant* (Montreal: Fides, 1944 [reprinted, 1967]), *Le Grand Marquis: Pierre de Rigaud de Vaudreuil, et la Louisiane*, 2nd ed. (Montreal: Fides, 1966), *La civilisation de la Nouvelle-France, 1713-1744* (Montreal: Fides, 1944), *François Bigot, Administrateur français*, 2 vols. (Montreal: Fides, 1948), and *La Guerre de la Conquête*, 2nd ed. (Montreal: Fides, 1966).

The nature of Canadian society before the conquest is bound to any discussion of the wars that preceded 1760. Cameron Nish, in "The Nature, Composition and Functions of the Canadian Bourgeoisie, 1729-1748," *CHA Report for 1966*, pp. 14-28, mentions many recent studies of this topic. Marcel Trudel's *The Seigneurial Regime* (Ottawa: Canadian Historical Association, 1956)* and Guy Frégault's *Canadian Society in the French Regime* (Ottawa: Canadian Historical Association, 1956)* are two brief summaries of a position challenging that typified by Francis Parkman's *The Old Régime in Canada* (Boston: Little, Brown, 1874). The newer interpretation has, in turn, been questioned by Jean Hamelin, *Economie et société en Nouvelle-France* (Quebec: Laval, 1960) and Fernand Ouellet's *Histoire economique et sociale du Quebec, 1760-1850* (Montreal: Fides, 1966). Another important work in this connection is Richard Colebrook Harris, *The Seigneurial System in Early Canada: A Geographical Study* (Quebec: Laval University Press, 1966).

Other books and articles of importance include:

Andrews, C. M. *The Colonial Period of American History*. 4 vols. (New Haven: Yale, 1934-8)*.

Barnes, V. F. *The Dominion of New England* (New Haven: Yale, 1923 [reprinted, New York: Ungar, 1960]).

Brebner, J. B. *New England's Outpost: Acadia before the Conquest of Canada* (New York: Columbia, 1927).

———. *The Explorers of North America, 1492-1806* (London: 1933 [reprinted, Cleveland: Meridian, 1964])*.

Bridenbaugh, Carl. *Cities in the Wilderness*. 2nd ed. (New York: Knopf, 1955)*.

———. *Cities in Revolt* (New York: Knopf, 1955)*.

Brunet, M. "The British Conquest: Canadian Social Scientists and the Fate of the *Canadiens*," *CHR*, XL (1959), pp. 93-107.

Crane, Verner W. *The Southern Frontier, 1670-1732* (Ann Arbor, Mich.: University of Michigan Press, 1929)*.

Cuneo, John R. *Robert Rogers of the Rangers* (New York: Oxford University Press, 1959).

Eccles, W. J. *Frontenac, The Courtier Governor* (Toronto: McClelland and Stewart, 1959)*.

──────. *Canada under Louis XIV, 1663-1701* (Toronto: McClelland and Stewart, 1964).

Flick, A. C. (ed.), *History of the State of New York*. 10 vols. (Albany: Friedman, 1933-37).

Frégault, Guy. "L'Empire britannique et la conquête du Canada, 1700-1713," *Revue d'histoire de l'Amérique française*, X (1956), pp. 153-82.

──────. "La Guerre de Sept Ans et la civilisation canadienne," *ibid.*, VII (1953-4), pp. 183-206.

Giraud, Marcel. *Histoire du Canada*. 2nd ed. (Paris: Presses universitaires de France, 1950).

Grant, W. L. "Canada Versus Guadeloupe: An Episode of the Seven Years' War," *AHR*, XVII (1911-12), pp. 735-43.

Greene, E. B. *Provincial America, 1690-1740* (New York: Harper, 1905 [reprinted, New York: Unger, 1964]).

Grinnell-Milne, Duncan. *Mad, Is He? The Character and Achievements of James Wolfe* (London: Bodley Head, 1963).

Hunt, G. T. *The Wars of the Iroquois* (Madison, Wis.: University of Wisconsin Press, 1940)*.

Innis, H. A. *The Fur Trade in Canada*. 2nd ed. (Toronto: University of Toronto Press, 1956)*.

Lawson, Murray G. *Fur: A Study in English Mercantilism, 1700-1775* (Toronto: University of Toronto Press, 1943).

Leach, Douglas E. *Flintlock and Tomahawk: New England in King Philip's War* (New York: Norton, 1958)*.

Lunn, J. E. "Agriculture and War in Canada, 1740-1760," *CHR*, XVI (1935), pp. 125-36.

Morton, Richard L. *Colonial Virginia*. 2 vols. (Chapel Hill, N.C.: University of North Carolina Press, 1960).

Pares, R. *War and Trade in the West Indies, 1739-1763* (Oxford: Clarendon, 1936 [reprint, London: Cass, 1963]).

—————. "American versus Continental Warfare, 1739-63," *EHR*, LI (1936), pp. 429-65.

Pargellis, Stanley M. *Lord Loudoun in North America* (New Haven: Yale, 1933 [reprinted, Hamden, Conn.: Shoe String, 1968]).

—————. "Braddock's Defeat," *AHR*, XLI (1936), pp. 253-69.

Parry, J. H. *The Establishment of European Hegemony, 1415-1715* (London, 1949 [reprinted, New York: Harper, 1963])*.

Rashed, Zenab E. *The Peace of Paris, 1763* (Liverpool: Liverpool University Press, 1951).

Rawlyk, G. A. *Yankees at Louisbourg* (Orono, Maine: University of Maine Press, 1967)*.

Reid, M. G. "Pitt's Decision to Keep Canada in 1761," *CHA Report for 1926*, pp. 21-36.

Rich, E. E. *The History of the Hudson's Bay Company, 1670-1870*. 2 vols. (London: Hudson Bay Record Society, 1958-60).

Savelle, Max. *The Diplomatic History of the Canadian Boundary, 1749-1763* (Toronto: Ryerson, 1940).

Schutz, John A. *William Shirley, King's Governor of Massachusetts* (Chapel Hill: University of North Carolina Press, 1961).

Sherrard, O. A. *Lord Chatham*. 3 vols. (London: Bodley Head, 1952-8).

Stacey, C. P. *Quebec, 1759; The Siege and the Battle* (Toronto: Macmillan, 1959).

Stanley, G. F. G. *Canada's Soldiers (1604-1954)* Toronto: Macmillan, 1954).

Trelease, A. W. *Indian Affairs in Colonial New York: The Seventeenth Century* (Ithaca, N.Y.: Cornell University Press, 1960).

Wainwright, N. B. *George Croghan, Wilderness Diplomat* (Chapel Hill: University of North Carolina Press, 1959).

Waller, G. M. *Samuel Vetch: Colonial Enterprizer* (Chapel Hill: University of North Carolina Press, 1960).

Zoltvany, Y. F. "The Problem of Western Policy under Phillipe de Rigaud de Vaudreuil, 1703-1725," *CHA Report for 1964*, pp. 9-24.

Index

Abenaquis: 19, 27, 42, 57, 67, 72, 93; attack New England, 18, 23, 38, 39, 51; reputation of, 25; expeditions against, 26; and Acadians, 51

Abercromby, Major-General James: 108, 113, 114; attacks Fort Carillon, 118-21

Acadia: 40, 41, 42, 44, 47, 58, 96, 102; and Canada's defence, 18; 'expulsion' from, 92-4

Adams, J. T.: re Phips expedition, 29

Aix-la-Chapelle, Peace of: 51, 67

Albany: 31, 32, 65, 73, 89, 101, 103, 108; and Leisler, 32-3; Albany conference, 73-4; *see also* Fur trade

Alcide: 78

Alexandria (Virginia): 82.

Algonquins: 23; *see also* individual tribes

Alleghany River: 53, 54.

American colonies: in 1689, 20-2; and Cartagena expedition, 45; balance of power with New France, 58; and French encirclement, 64-5; in 1755, 71-4; raids on (1756), 98; and Pitt's offensive, 114-5; *see also* individual colonies

American Revolution: 131, 132

Amherst, Major-General Jeffrey: 1, 113 126; at Louisbourg, 118

Andros, Sir Edmund: 32

Annapolis Royal: 47, 51; *see also* Port Royal

Anville, Jean-Baptiste-Louis-Frédéric de La Rochefoucauld, duc d': 50-1

Appalachians: 53

Austria: ends alliance with Britain, 74, 79

Barcelona: English attack, 30

Bart, Jean: 13

Beachy Head: French victory at, 13

Beaujeu, Daniel-Hyacinthe-Marie de: 85

Bigot, Francois: and fall of Canada, 69-70

Blainville, Pierre-Joseph de Céloron de: expedition to Ohio Valley, 53-4

Blenheim: battle of, 11

Board of Trade, British: 92

Boscawen, Vice-Admiral Edward: 77n; to Gulf of St. Lawrence (1775), 77-8, 94; Lagos Bay (1759), 126

Boston: 18, 22, 25, 26, 51; wartime prosperity of, 23

Braddock, Major-General Edward: 63, 66, 72, 82, 94, 97, 98, 122, 132; to aid Virginia, 75; expedition of, 2, 76, 84-7, 88; "offensive" of, objectives, 82-3, forces in, 82-4, types of warfare in, 82-4, cost of, 94, significance of, 94-6

Bradstreet, Lieutenant-Colonel John: attacks Fort Frontenac, 121-2

Britain: and Walker expedition, 39-40; and Peace of Utrecht, 40-1; and 'uneasy peace,' 43-4, 45; and Louisbourg (1745), 49-50; and Ohio clash, 55, 75-6; and New World (1755), 75-8; and Braddock's offensive, 82-4, 90; and Acadians, 92-4; and 1756 campaign, 94-5; commitment to America in 1758, 114-6; naval blockade, 110, 123-4, 134; and Peace of Paris, 129-31

Brunet, Michel: 1

Canada (New France): 3, 4, 17, 20, 25, 26, 33, 35, 42, 57, 58, 68, 74, 101-2, 109, 123, 126; in 1689, 13-20; Phips and, 26-30; seizes initiative (1692-7), 37-8; and Peace of Utrecht, 40-1; reasons for survival, 41-2; military objectives of, 42; and Ohio Valley, 53-7; condition in 1755, 63-71; and Braddock's defeat, 84-5; renewed raids from, 97-8; and Vaudreuil's offensive, 97-110; feud over military strategy, 101-2, 103-6, 108; and Fort William Henry 'massacre,' 103-8; in 1758, 123-4; in 1759, 125-7; surrender of, 128; vs. Guadeloupe, 130-1

Canso: 46-7, 57

Cape Ann: 23

Carolinas: 21, 71; North, 55, 84; South, 57, 84

Cartagena: 12, 45

Casco: 18, 38

Cataracoui: *see* Fort Frontenac

Catawba: 84

Champlain, Samuel de: 1, 4

Chaudiére River: 63, 72

Cherokee: 84

Chignecto, Isthmus of: 92, 93

Choiseul, Etienne-Francois, duc de: and Peace of Paris, 130-1

Church, Benjamin: 26; sent against Abenaquis, 26, 39

Clark, Lieutenant Matthew: 120

Colbert, Jean-Baptiste: 12-13, 80
Connecticut: 21, 23; and Winthrop's expedition, 34
Convention of Kloster-Zeven: 111
Coureurs de bois: 19, 70
Cumberland, William Augustus, Duke of: 111, 112, 116; and British military plans (1756), 94-5
Deerfield (Mass.): 23, 42, 57; raided, 11, 38-9
Dafoe, Daniel: maxims of war, 6
Delancey, James: 88
Delawares: 53
Denonville, Jacques-René de Brisay, marquis de: attack on Senecas, 16
Dieskau, General Jean-Armand, baron de: 66, 80; and Battle of Lake George, 91-2
Dinwiddie, Lieutenant-Governor Robert: 75, 122; and Braddock, 84-5
Dominion of New England: 24; and American colonial unity, 21-2
Drucour, Augustin de: defends Louisbourg, 118
Dubois, Abbé Guilliaume: 43
Duguay-Trouin, Réné: 13
Dumas, Captain Jean-Daniel: 97, 108
Dummer's War: 44
Dunbar, Colonel Thomas: 88, 97
Dunkirk: 78
Duquesne, Governor-General Ange, marquis: 54, 67, 79
Easton, Treaty of: 122
Eccles, W. J.: 15
Egg Island: 42
England: and American war 1689, 11-13; and Treaty of Ryswick, 38; *see* Britain
Eyre, Colonel William: 105
Fleury, André-Hercule, Cardinal: 43
Forbes, General John: 113, 122-3
Fort Altamaha: built, 45
Fort Beauséjour: 96, 113; and Braddock's offensive, 82-3; fall of, 92-3
Fort Bull: 99, 103
Fort Carillon: 2, 64, 66, 101, 102, 106, 109, 114, 121, 122, 126, 133; defense of, 118-121
Fort Chambly: 34, 66
Fort Cumberland: 97
Fort Duquesne: 55, 65, 72, 74, 82, 108, 113, 114, 124; built, 54; and Braddock, 84-8; falls, 98, 122-3
Fort Edward: 90, 91, 103, 107, 108
Fort Frontenac: 65, 90, 114; falls, 121-2
Fort Gaspereau: 92, 93
Fort Lawrence: 93

Fort Le Boeuf: 54, 55
Fort Massachusetts: taken (1747), 51
Fort Miamis: 53
Fort Necessity: 65, 75; capture of, 55-7
Fort Niagara: 66, 113, 121, 126; and Braddock, 82; and Shirley, 88-90
Fort Nicholson: 64
Fort Oswego: 45; and Shirley, 88-90; falls (1756), 99-101
Fort St. Frédéric: 45, 51, 63, 64, 66, 94, 102, 113, 126; and Johnson, 82-3, 90-2
Fort Venango: 54
Fort William Henry (Maine): 38
Fort William Henry (New York): 2, 64, 69; campaign against, 103-8; massacre at, 107-8
Fortescue, J. W.: on Abercromby, 120
Fox, Henry: 95
France: 3, 15, 39, 58, 64, 116, 121; and American war (1689), 11-13; and Peace of Ryswick, 38; *entente* with Britain, 43-5; and Aix-la-Chapelle, 51; on Ohio, 53-5; aid to Canada (1755), 66, (1757), 102, (1759-60), 123-4; and American war (1755), 78-81; strategy of, 76-7, 110; and Peace of Paris, 130, 131
Frederick II the Great, King of Prussia: 74, 129
Frégault, Guy: 3; on Montcalm, 120
'French Canadian': meaning of, 2
Frontenac, Louis de Baude, comte de: 4, 35, 49, 57
Fur trade: Canadian, 17, 19, 67, 68-9; New York, 31-3, 41, 54; of Ohio valley, 53, 54; *see also* Albany, Hudson Bay
Gabarus Bay: landing at (1758), 116-7
Gage, Lieutenant-Colonel Thomas: 85
Georgia: 45; founding, 43-4
George II, King of England: 46, 76; aggressive policy of, 129
George III, King of England: 129-31
Gibraltar: 30, 115
Gipson, Lawrence Henry: 3, 108*n*
Graham, G. S.: 79*n*, 127-8
Grande Société,: 69-70
Grand Pré: 51
Great Miami River: 53
Guadeloupe: raided (1691), 12; vs. Canada, 130-1
Gulf of St. Lawrence: 28, 126
Halifax: 92
Hanover: 115, 129; and English politics, 76

Hardwicke, Philip Yorke, Earl of: 111
Havana: 129
Haviland, Lieutenant-Colonel William: 128
Hawke, Admiral Sir Edward: 123
Hébert, Louis: 1
Hendrick, Chief: 63; and Johnson's expedition, 90; killed, 91
Hocquart, Gilles: 68, 68n
Howe, Captain Richard: 78, 78n
Hudson Bay: 36, 38, 40; Company, 69
Hudson River: 18, 31, 64, 72, 101, 103, 108, 109
Hurons: 17
Iberville, Pierre Le Moyne d': 13, 38
Ile Royale: 130
Illinois: 17, 19, 69
Illinois River: 53
Indians: the term, 2-3; and Canada (1689), 19, 25, 27; and Massachusetts, 25-6; and Ohio valley struggle, 53-7; and Canada (1755), 66-8; and Braddock, 84-5; raid American west frontier, 97-8; and Fort William Henry (1757), 107-8; and Bradstreet, 121; and Forbes, 122; join British, 126, 128; *see also* individual tribes and Warfare, guerilla.
Iroquois: 19, 26, 33, 35, 42, 67, 72, 82; threaten Canada, 17; raid Lachine, 19; Canadians attack, 36; and Peace of Utrecht, 40; tacit neutrality of, 42; at Albany Conference, 73; rejoin British, 126; *see also* Mohawks; Onandagas; Oneidas; Senecas
Jacobites: 43
James II, King of England: 21, 22, 32
Johnson, Sir William: 82, 95, 126; appointed Indian agent, 73; and Shirley, 88-9; expedition of, 90-2
Jumonville, Joseph Coulon de Villiers, sieur de: 'assassinated,' 55, 59
Kennebec River: 25, 51, 72
Keppel, Admiral Augustus: 82
King George's War: *see* War of the Austrian Succession
King Philip's War: 25, 34; effect on Mass., 25-6
King William's War: *see* War of the League of Augsburg
Lachine: raided, 19
La Galissonière, Roland-Michel Barrin, comte de: 65, 67, 80n
Lagos Bay: naval battle in, 77n, 126
La Hogue: naval Battle at, 13

La Jonquiére, Pierre-Jacques de Taffanel, marquis de: 67
Lake Champlain: 17, 23, 34, 101, 109, 114, 116
Lake Erie: 54, 64
Lake George: 64, 81, 114; battle of, 90-2; barges destroyed on, 106-7
Lake Ontario: command of, 88, 109, 114, 121
La Motte, Admiral comte du Bois de: 78, 80, 116
La Prairie: attacked by Schuyler, 34-5
La Salle, Réné-Robert, chevalier, sieur de: 4
Lanctôt, Gustave: 3, 107n
Lawrence, Lieutenant-Governor Charles: 93-4
Lévis, François-Gaston, chevalier: 119, 127-8
Leisler, Captain Jacob: seizes power in New York, 32; in power, 32-5; deposed, 35
Le Loutre, abbé Jean-Louis: 51
Ligonier, Field-Marshal John, Earl: 113
Loudoun, John Campbell, Earl of: 95, 100, 102, 103, 105, 113, 116; army under, 101; removed, 112; plan for 1758, 114
Louis XIV, King of France: 12, 13, 43, 130
Louis XV, King of France: 43
Louisbourg: 58, 63, 64, 65, 66, 68, 72, 92, 102, 115, 126, 129; started, 45; captured (1745), 46-51; attack planned (1757), 114; captured (1758), 116-118
Louisiana: 44, 64, 65
Madras: 51, 129
Maine: frontier, 18, 23, 51
Marin, Lieutenant Joseph: 106
Marlborough, John Churchill, Duke of: 39, 41; opposed to colonial expeditions, 11-12
Maryland: 21, 57, 71, 82, 109; raided, 97-8
Massachusetts: 18, 21, 35, 36, 49, 82; in 1689, 22-6; military organization, 25-6; and Phips' expeditions, 26-30; renewed offensive against Canada, 39, 42; raided, 51; *see also* New England
Mather, Cotton: 2; on war with Canada, 24, 27; on war and evil spirits, 25
Miamis: 19, 53; settlement destroyed, 54

Micmacs: 51, 67, 93
Mingos: 53, 84
Minorca: 75, 130
Mohawks: 35, 38; *see* Iroquois
Monckton, Colonel Robert: expedition led by, 72, 93, 94, 96
Monongahela, Battle of: 81, 84-7, 90, 91
Montcalm, Louis-Joseph, marquis de: 66, 78, 127, 133; and Oswego campaign, 100-101; on colonial war, 101, 109; vs. Vaudreuil, 101-2, 103-6, 110, 118; and Fort William Henry campaign, 106-8; defensive strategy of, 109-10; defense of Fort Carillon, 118-21; on fall of Fort Frontenac, 122; predicts fall of Canada, 124
Montreal: 18, 64, 65, 101, 109, 114; surrender at, 126, 128
Munro, Lieutenant-Colonel George: surrenders Fort William Henry, 107
Murray, Brigadier-General James: 126, 128; and battle of Ste. Foy, 127
Neale, Daniel: on Phips' expedition, 29
New England: 38, 58; and Phips, 26, 30; takes Port Royal, 39; and failure of Walker expedition, 40; and attack on Louisbourg, 49, 50; *see also* Maine, Massachusetts, and New Hampshire
New Hampshire: 18, 23, 51
New Jersey: 122; screened from war, 21
New Orleans: founded, 45
New York: 18, 21, 26, 36, 39, 54, 71, 75, 82, 84; in 1689, 31-6; Dutch in, 31-2; military objectives of, 42
Newcastle, Thomas Pelham-Holles, Duke of: 75, 76, 79, 111
Newfoundland: Franco-Canadian attack, 36; d'Iberville raid, 38; ceded to Britain, 40
Nova Scotia: *see* Acadia
Nicholson, Lieutenant-Governor Francis: on Canadian intentions (1689), 32
Ohio Company of Virginia: formation of, 52, 53
Ohio Valley: 53-7, 58, 63, 64, 67, 72, 109
Onandagas: 38; *see also* Iroquois
Oneidas: 38; *see also* Iroquois
Orléans, Philippe, duc d': 43
Oswego: 2, 121; captured (1756), 69, 99-101
Oswego River: 99; difficult descent of, 88

Ottawas: Canadian allies, 17; capture of Lake George barges, 106
Oyster Bay (New Hampshire): 38
Paris, Peace of (1763): and Canada, 129-31
Parkham, Francis: on Anglo-Saxon superiority, 4; on 'uneasy peace,' 45; on Fort William Henry, 105
Peckham, Howard H.: on feudal nature of New France, 4, 14
Pennsylvania: 54, 71, 74, 82, 109, 122; and war (1689), 20-1; and Ohio rivalry, 57; raided, 97-8; goes to war, 98
Pepperell, Sir William: and Louisbourg, 1, 49; relations with Warren, 50; in Shirley's expedition, 89
Philadelphia: 71
Phillipines: capture of, 129
Phips, Sir William: 1, 2, 35, 40, 58; background of, 26; captures Port Royal, 27; attacks Quebec, 28-30
Pichon, Thomas: 93
Pickawillany: destroyed, 54
Pitt, William: 69, 116, 121, 126; to power, 111-3; and army, 112-3; plan for 1758, 113-4; reasons for success, 114-6; on Peace of Paris, 129-30
Plains of Abraham, Battle of: significance of, 1, 124-5
Port Royal: 26, 42, 50, 58; as base for privateers, 18-9; attacked (1690), 27, (1707), 39, (1710), 39, *see also* Annapolis Royal
Pownall, Thomas: on Canadian Indian policy, 67-8
Presqu'Ile: founded, 54
Prideaux, Brigadier-General John: 126
Prussia: British subsidy for, 115, 130; estranged from Britain, 131
Quebec: 35, 42, 58, 64, 65, 66, 92, 102, 106, 109, 115, 116, 124, 126, 133; Phips at, 28-30; Walker and, 40; planned attack (1746), 50; Wolfe at, 124-5; Lévis' siege, 127-8
Queen Anne's War *see* War of the Spanish Succession
Quiberon Bay: battle in, 128
Raystown (Penn.): 122
Richelieu River: 63, 72, 101, 128
Rochefort: 50, 123
Rogers, Robert: 90; rangers of, 83, 90, 128
Ryswick, Peace of: 43, 51; negotiation of, 12; terms of, 38

Saco (Maine): raided (1703), 38
St. John, Henry: reasons for the Walker expedition, 39-40; and Peace of Utrecht, 41
St. Lawrence River: 64, 128, 130; and Walker expedition, 40; blockaded, 68
Ste. Foy, Battle of: significance of, 127-8
Salem (Mass.): 23; witch trials, 25, 30
Salmon Falls (N.H.): 17
Sandusky Bay: fort built, 54
Saratoga: burned by Canadians, 51
Schenectady (N.Y.): 17, 32; raided (1690), 31; avenged, 35
Schuyler, Captain John: leads raid on Canada, 34-5
Schuyler, Peter, Mayor of Albany; and raid on Canada, 35
Senecas: 53; *see also* Iroquois
Shawnees: 53, 84
Shirley, Governor William: 94, 95, 100, 121; and Louisbourg (1745), 49; warned of French plans, 51; on French encirclement, 64-5; expedition of, 88-90; and Acadians, 93
Société du Canada: 69, 70
Spain: 39, 45, 129
Springfield (Mass.): 23
Stacey, C. P.: on fall of New France, 127
Stanhope, James Earl: 43
Ticonderoga: *see* Fort Carillon
Townshend, Brigadier-General George: 125
Utrecht, Peace of: 51, 63, 131; terms of, 40-1; aftermath of, 43-5
Vaudreuil, François-Pierre de Rigaud de: 100; at Oswego, 100; attacks Fort William Henry, 104-5, 106
Vaudreuil, Governor Pierre de Rigaud, marquis de: 66, 91, 119, 122, 133; rift with Montcalm, 101-6, 118, 120; his offensive, 97-110, 123; strategy of, 109-10; surrenders New France, 128
Vernon, Admiral Edward: and Cartagena expedition, 45
Virginia: 21, 71, 82, 84, 88, 109, 122; into the Ohio Valley, 53-7; enters struggle with New France, 59; receives Brit ishsupport, 74; raided from west, 97-8
Walker, Admiral Hovenden; expedition of, 12, 28, 39-40, 42, 58
Walley, Major John: and assault of Quebec, 28-30

Walpole, Sir Robert: 43
Warfare: patterns of (to 1755), 57-9 (after 1755), 63, 96; types of, 5-7, combined, 99-101, 103-6, 114-5, confused, 55-7, 92, 107-8, contest between, 7, 109-10, 123, 128, 132-3; *see also* Montcalm; Vaudreuil; warfare, conventional; warfare, guerilla
Warfare, conventional: described, 6-7; Mass. and, 25-7; and Louisbourg (1745), 49; in Ohio Valley, 55-7; and Braddock's offensive, 82-7, 95-6; at Fort William Henry, 107; at Fort Carillon, 118-21; triumph of, 123, 128, 132-4
Warfare, guerilla: described, 6-7; fur trade and, 17; in Ohio Valley, 55-7; and Braddock, 82-5; and Johnson's expedition, 90-2; in Acadia, 93; defence and, 124; eclipse of, 123, 128, 132-4
War of the Austrian Succession: 11, 45, 63, 67; in America, 46-52
War of the League of Augsburg: 11; in America, 26-38
War of the Spanish Succession: 11; in America, 38-43
Warren; Commodore Peter: at Louisbourg, 49-50; and Pepperell, 50
Washington, George: to Fort Le Boeuf, 54-5; and 'assassination' of Jumonville, 55; and Fort Necessity, 55-7, 67, 75; and frontier defence, 98
Webb, Major-General Daniel: 107
Wells (Maine): raided (1692), 38 (1703), 38
Westfield (Mass.): 23
West Indies: 12, 26, 68, 129, 130
William of Orange, Stadtholder of Netherlands: invades England, 22
Wills Creek (Va.): 53
Willson, Beckles: on battle of Plains of Abraham, 124
Winter Harbour (Maine): raided (1703), 38
Winthrop, Fitz-John: background of, 34; expedition of, 34-5
Wolfe, Major-General James: 1, 69; at Louisbourg, 117; at Quebec, 124-5; authorizes vengeance on Canadians, 128
Wraxall, Peter: on Johnson's army, 95
Yamassee War: 44
York (Maine): raided, 38